EL CHAPO

EL CHAPO

The Story of the World's Most Notorious Drug Lord

Terry Burrows

PICTURE CREDITS

p.22, 55: **Alamy Stock Photo**
All other images: **Getty Images**

This edition published in 2021 by Arcturus Publishing Limited
26/27 Bickels Yard, 151–153 Bermondsey Street,
London SE1 3HA

AD007824US

Printed in the UK

CONTENTS

INTRODUCTION

The rich narrative surrounding the world of Joaquín 'El Chapo' Guzmán Loera can be viewed through so many classic storytelling tropes that it's no surprise to find countless people the world over with a fascination for his endlessly complex unfolding tale. Indeed, there are those who seem to have followed the events of his life with an almost fanlike zeal. For this is an age-old, rags-to-riches saga. He's the poor, semi-literate boy with the big dream. The young man born on the wrong side of the tracks, who becomes one of the richest men in the world. And he's the cunning outlaw who outwits the authorities time and time again, escaping from maximum-security prisons not just once but twice; and using methods – buried under a pile of bed linen in the laundry trolley, burrowing out through a 1 mile/1.6 km-long underground tunnel – that any serious crime novelist would dismiss as crass or implausible. Now in his 60s, El Chapo Guzmán looks set to spend the rest of his life in a US prison cell, but how many of us secretly thrill at the idea that he might yet conjure up a third audacious jailbreak?

So what's behind this curiosity? Why is it that in 2014, the day after El Chapo was captured for the second time, the hashtag #FreeElChapo trended on social media? Why the fascination with Mexico's infamous narco villains and the quasi-paramilitary organizations they lead? For most of us, the appeal is simply that of a gripping, constantly unfurling drama, one whose meandering twists and turns never cease to surprise.

There are the constantly shifting landscapes of Mexico's drug cartels; the rise and fall of the bosses – the *capos* – and their lieutenants, most of whom eventually end up dead or in prison. Then there are the alliances. The betrayals. The absurd opulence of their lifestyles. The fleets of luxury cars and gold-plated AK-47s. Even in death, their most celebrated corpses are laid to rest in multi-million-dollar mausoleums. And all this even before we turn to their would-be nemeses – the United States Drugs Enforcement Agency (DEA) and the Mexican authorities. The latter evidently include among their number *many* who have accepted cash-filled suitcases handed over by a 'lawyer' representing one of the cartels. You really *couldn't* make this stuff up.

It's easy to romanticize the actions of figures like El Chapo. The more we read about them in books and magazines, and see them dramatized on our TV screens, the more difficult it becomes to separate the myth from the fact. *Of course* we know that these are unequivocally 'bad' people. But perhaps even this is more nuanced than it may at first appear. In a country where over half of its citizens – more than 63 million people – live below what even the Mexican government views as the poverty line, there are many for whom El Chapo *is* a heroic figure. He is one of their own, the boy who escaped the hardship of the Sierra Madre mountains and made good. When the government had forgotten about them, he was the benefactor who provided work in the poppy fields and marijuana plantations, the meth labs, cocaine smuggling or the cartel's private security forces. He provided food for the elderly and toys for the children. Even during the Covid-19 pandemic, parcels were distributed to the vulnerable with the image of his face on the box.

To fully accept this line of thinking, of course, requires suspension of too many unavoidable basic facts. Many of those living in rural poverty who work for the drug cartels have no other real choice. And in among the romance, it *is* easy to forget that we are talking about a mercilessly violent murderer – a man whose wealth has been used to corrupt the highest levels of Mexico's government, judicial system, police and military. At the conclusion of Guzmán's trial in 2019, prosecuting attorney Robert Capers denounced him as no 'do-gooder or Robin Hood' but 'a small cancerous tumour that metastasized into a full-blown scourge'.

We should not forget that this was a man prepared to sanction the kidnapping, grotesque tortures and brutal murders of anyone who got in the way of his business objectives. Nor that his business earned its vast wealth by flooding America and the rest of the world with cocaine, heroin, fentanyl and crystal meth.

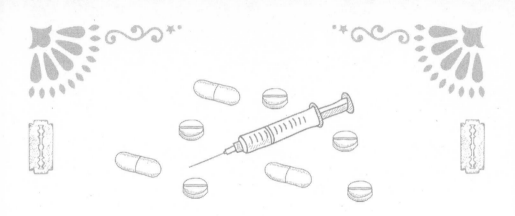

CHAPTER 1:
MEETING A DEMAND

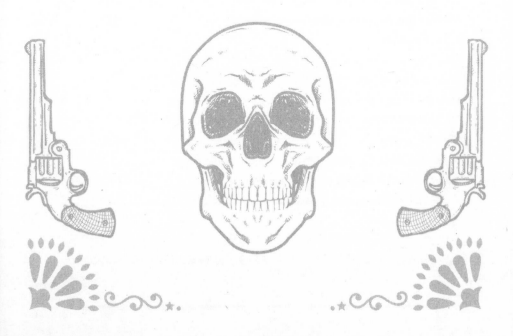

Con cuerno de chivo y bazooka en la nuca
Volando cabezas a quien se atravieza
Somos sanguinarios, locos bien ondeados
Nos gusta matar
Pa' dar levantones, somos los mejores
Siempre en caravana, toda mi plebada
Bien empecherados, blindados y listos
Para ejecutar

With an AK-47 and bazooka at the neck
Heads flying off anyone who dares
We're bloodthirsty madmen
We like to kill
We're the best for kidnapping
Always with a group, all my homeboys
With bulletproof vests, armed and ready
To execute

'*Sanguinarios del M1*' – '*narcorrido*' by El Movimiento Alterado

S ince the mid-20th century the trade in, and common use of, illegal narcotics has proved to be one of the most controversial and vexing subjects within the western world. It has always enraged establishment opinion. Almost 50 years of America's 'War on Drugs' has cost the country billions of dollars and yet it appears to have been lost – or at least it has yielded few tangible positive results. As the US authorities discovered a century ago during the age of Prohibition, one direct consequence has been the emergence of powerful 'drug lords', possessing unimaginable personal wealth and with enough covert influence to sway national governments.

At the centre of this problem lies one incontrovertible fact. Regardless of the ethical or legal line toed by the moral guardians of the West, there is a massive global demand for illicit narcotics: for cocaine, heroin, ecstasy, black-market prescription opioids and, in those places where it remains illegal, marijuana.

Both suppliers and consumers are evidently prepared to risk criminal prosecution as they go about their business. In 2013, America's National Institute on Drug Abuse published research that raised more than a few eyebrows when it suggested that 9.4 per cent of Americans over the age of 12 had consumed an illicit drug during the previous month. That's a whole lot of law-breakers – 24.6 million of them, in fact.

Such volumes, of course, illustrate the sheer scale of the illegal drug business. Although detailed figures are impossible to come by, estimates suggest an industry worth over $400 billion (£320bn) annually; indeed, America's Office of National Drug Policy reported that in 2013 $100 billion (£80bn) was spent on illegal narcotics in the USA alone. So vast is this commercial enterprise that it is surpassed by only the arms and oil industries.

Little wonder, then, that over time the producers and suppliers of Central America – from which region a significant proportion of the world's drug trade emanates – should evolve into large-scale, sophisticated organizations with wealth and influence to rival some of the mightiest legal business empires.

It was within this environment that a brutal drug 'kingpin' like 'El Chapo' Guzmán Loera was able to reinvent himself. Like numerous young Mexicans before and since, Guzmán grew up in rural poverty as he sought to eke out a meagre living first as a teenage *gomeros*, or opium farmer, and then as a low-level marijuana dealer. Yet by the time he had reached his mid-30s, through a combination of wild ambition, smart business acumen... and the most appallingly brutal violence, Guzmán was head of Mexico's powerful and ruthless Sinaloa drug cartel, an organization he had helped create in the late-1980s.

During that time, Guzmán accrued a personal fortune of $14 billion (£11bn) and, to his evident pride, even secured a place on the annual Forbes global billionaires list.

It's mind-boggling that such widespread illegal business activities should have been allowed to exist, let alone flourish untamed. And yet millions fall within the industry's global employ, from subsistence-level village farmers in Afghanistan, Pakistan, Guatemala, Mexico and Colombia – all of whom rely on the harvesting of opium poppies for their living – to logistics experts able to circumvent international borders, and hierarchies of dealers on the street who supply the end-users.

A LAW UNTO THEMSELVES

In Mexico, the power and wealth of the drug cartels are so vast that they have become a vital part of the nation's economy. With 500 towns and cities in Mexico actively engaged in the trafficking of drugs across the border into the United States, almost half a million people are employed directly by the Mexican drug organizations themselves, the biggest of which in recent times have been the Sinaloa and Los Zetas cartels who cover the Northwest and the US border, the Jalisco New Generation cartel in the central Tierra Caliente region and the Gulf cartel on the southern border.

Unsurprisingly, given the vast wealth and numbers of individuals involved, these have developed into sophisticated modern organizations,

File photo of El Chapo Guzmán at La Palma maximum-security prison in Almaloya, Juárez on 10 July 1993. Gang members smuggled in cash, allowing Guzmán to bribe prison officers and effectively to run his expanding drug empire from his cell.

characterized by a formal chain of command with clearly defined levels of authority and responsibility just like any other corporation.

Many of the cartels and their leaders have become household names on the global stage. Often operating beyond the reach of national law-enforcement agencies, they are effectively the law in some parts of Central America, infamously meting out their own rough justice to those who pose a threat to their business activities, be they the police, the military, rival cartels or even transgressors within their own ranks. Statistics produced in 2012 by the government of President Felipe Calderón suggested that more than 60,000 deaths had resulted from the peak years of Mexico's drug wars; critics contested the figure, saying that it was less than half the real number, with a further 27,000 estimated to be among the 'missing'.

The brutality of the cartels is, of course, legendary, with executions regularly carried out on a grand scale in the most gruesome fashion imaginable. Sometimes these have seen sadism, barbarity and cruelty on a grand scale, acting as a warning to those who might be considering crossing the gangs.

A typical example took place in Michoacán on 8 August 2019, when members of the Jalisco New Generation cartel beheaded nine members of rival gang Los Viagras. Their naked bodies were hung from a high bridge alongside a giant banner that declared: *Haz patria y mata a un Viagra* ('Be a patriot, kill a Viagra'). The shocking photographs were widely published in the world's media.

HEROES AND VILLAINS

In spite of the frequent horrific violence, drug cartel leaders are frequently viewed in a positive light within their home territories. This is not surprising since they often provide a basic living for some of the region's most impoverished rural citizens. In some cases, this is the difference between survival and starvation. Pablo Escobar, head of the Medellín cartel which once dominated the global cocaine trade, was regarded by many Colombians as one their country's greatest-ever philanthropists.

In the 1980s, he built hospitals, sports stadiums and homes for the poor; he became so popular that he was even elected to Colombia's congress. When the scale of his criminal activities became officially known, he is said to have offered to pay off his country's $10 billion (£8bn) national debt in exchange for immunity from extradition. (It's likely, in fact, that Escobar had simply accrued more cash than he was able to handle. His brother Roberto, who acted as the Medellín cartel's chief accountant, would later reveal how cash was simply hidden away in remote fields and crumbling warehouses. 'Pablo was earning so much that each year we would write off 10 per cent of the money because the rats would eat it in storage or it would be damaged by water or lost.')

To the great annoyance of the Mexican authorities, drug lords like El Chapo have found themselves featuring heavily in popular culture. Global television series such as *Narcos* and *El Chapo* – both fictionalized accounts of the Central American drugs trade – were watched by audiences of millions across the globe. Even if their most brutal and vile exploits are exposed on screen, some would argue that these shows are guilty of both publicizing and, to an extent, 'bigging up' some of the most violent criminals in recent history.

In Mexico itself, the deeds of El Chapo and his ilk have found their way into popular song known as *narcorridos* – *narco corridos* ('drug ballads'). Although these songs sometimes sound like an innocent mix of mariachi and polka, they chronicle and often glorify the world of the illegal drugs industry. Grammy-winner Gerardo Ortiz's 'El Primer Ministro' famously celebrated in song how a poor El Chapo Guzmán built a mighty empire from nothing.

The song *'Sanguinarios del M1'* ('Bloodthirsty M1') by vocal collective Movimiento Alterado (Altered Movement) pulls no punches in its depiction of life in the cartels: *Bien empecherados, blindados y listos, para ejecutar* (With bulletproof vests, armed and ready to execute); Alfredo

Rios, group member and star in his own right, better known as 'El Ko-mander', has even admitted that he submitted lyrics for clearance by the Sinaloa cartel before they were recorded! 'People love listening to stories from bad people,' he declared to *VICE News* in 2013. 'They eventually convert them to their own heroes. I am not sure why, but it's so good to see people from the hood get wealthy and powerful no matter what.'

This is, however, a musical genre fraught with peril. Singer Diego Rivas discovered that glorifying one cartel leader was just as apt to antagonize one of his rivals: his most famous song, *'Homenaje al Chapo Guzmán'* ('Homage to Chapo Guzmán'), declared that *Es bajito de estatura, pero su cerebro es grande* ('He is short of stature, but his brain is large'). It continued, *Si se presentan problemas, con cuernos de chivo hay que responder* ('If there's a problem you respond with goat horns' – Mexican criminal slang for an AK-47 rifle, referring to the curved shape of its magazine clip).

The song even namechecks El Chapo's most noted lieutenant, 'Licienciado' (Dámaso López Nuñez). On 12 November 2011 in the city of Culiacán deep in Sinaloa territory, Rivas and two of his friends perished in a drive-by shooting thought to have been an execution by the Los Zetas cartel. Rivas is just one of a number of well-known Mexican musicians to have been caught up in drug violence who found themselves at the wrong end of the goat's horns.

EVOLUTION OF THE DRUG ROUTES

Long before the birth of the first Mexican drug cartels, the country's geographical location made it an obvious staging and transhipment point for the trafficking of every type of contraband into the United States. Mexican bootleggers had provided alcohol during the Prohibition era and many of the same criminal organizations would later bring heroin and marijuana into the country.

By the 1970s, these well-established networks enabled Pablo Escobar's Colombian Medellín cartel to dominate the global supply of cocaine. Using local expertise in the logistics of smuggling and transportation,

Escobar – the first of the 'superstar' drug barons – formed partnerships with a number of Mexican gangs.

Initially, they were given large cash payments to deal with the shipments of narcotics across the US border, but as they grew in wealth and power during the 1980s, they began to take their payments in cocaine itself. This would usually amount to around 40 per cent of the total shipment, which they would then proceed to traffic themselves. Eventually, with the capture and assassination of Escobar in 1993 and the collapse of the Medellín group, organizations like the Gulf cartel and Guzmán's own Sinaloa cartel stepped in to pick up the slack.

Traditionally, the Mexican cartels have functioned much in the same way as the Mafia 'families' of New York and Chicago in the middle of the 20th century; territorial boundaries were tenuously agreed to facilitate trade, but more often than not these would break down as the various parties lapsed into bitter internecine warfare.

From the earliest of days, the balance of power among the Mexican cartels shifted continually even if gangs largely kept to their own domains. Violence would periodically break out when arrests or executions created sudden power vacuums, or when cartels splintered and new organizations emerged.

By and large, however, until the late-1980s widespread political corruption allowed for tacit agreements to be forged between the main cartels and Mexico's governing Partido Revolucionario Institucional (PRI, or Institutional Revolutionary Party) which managed to create an uneasy peace. Although Mexico's government was publicly at war with the drugs industry, bribery and corruption at the highest levels allowed the cartels to go about their business without too much hindrance.

By 1990, the PRI had held power for 60 years, having been created in 1929 by the heads of the military in the wake of the Mexican Revolution. An authoritarian one-party regime, it was famously described by writer Mario Vargas Llosa as 'the perfect dictatorship, because it is a camouflaged dictatorship'.

From its earliest days, Mexico's military was incorporated into the structure of the party as a means of asserting control over the civilian population. This was demonstrated dramatically on the global stage in 1968 when 10,000 pro-democracy protesters – most of them school or university students – gathered peacefully on the streets of Mexico City. They were met by gunfire from government troops in what is now remembered as the Tlatelolco massacre. Official reports state that 44 were killed, but the true figure is thought to have been closer to 400. It was to be a turning point in Mexican history and resulted in much of the country's middle class turning against the PRI.

As a consequence, by the end of the 1980s other political parties began to gain in popularity. The PRI, meanwhile, was denounced as corrupt – electoral fraud, voter suppression and violence against other parties were by this time widely believed to be rife. Elections, the party's critics argued, were provided merely to create the appearance of democracy. And, what's more, the connection between the party – and thus parts of the government – and the drug cartels was becoming increasingly evident.

In the early 1980s, Manuel Buendía, a journalist and political columnist working for Mexico's popular *Excélsior* newspaper, began investigating links between government officials and drug trafficking. His findings further led him to believe that the United States Central Intelligence Agency (the CIA) might also have been complicit. His controversial reports angered many of Mexico's politicians and business leaders. On 30 May 1984, Buendía was gunned down in Mexico City while leaving his office; members of the country's elite police force, the Federal Security Directorate, would later be charged with the killing.

WIDESPREAD VIOLENCE

Proof that corruption went all the way to the pinnacle of government later emerged when it was discovered that General Jesús Gutiérrez Rebollo, the head and public face of President Zedillo's specially created anti-drug unit, had been taking payments from the Juárez cartel in exchange for 'closing his eyes' to their activities.

The PRI's influence rapidly waned during the 1990s and it eventually lost control of the country in the 2000 election when President Vicente Fox brought the right-wing PAN party to power. He publicly vowed to begin Mexico's first significant crackdown on the drug cartels.

The first major outbreak of warfare between the rival drug organizations followed the arrest of Gulf cartel leader Osiel Cárdenas Guillén in 2003. This led directly to a challenge from El Chapo Guzmán's Sinaloa cartel for supremacy over the coveted Texas corridor. A second bloody dispute between Sinaloa and the Juárez cartels saw El Chapo emerge as victor. The scale of violence startled Mexico's leaders when they were told that an estimated 12,000 lives had been lost in the fighting.

A similar explosion of violence in Michoacana saw the birth of a splinter group, La Familia, emerging from the allied Gulf and Los Zetas cartels. In 2006, the new president, Felipe Calderón, despatched 6,500 Mexican troops to the region in an effort to control the violence. This ushered in a period widely known as the Mexican Drug Wars, which continues to play out to the present day.

As Calderón increased his military involvement – there are still almost 50,000 troops engaged in Mexico's anti-drug policy – he achieved significant public successes in capturing high-ranking drug lords. Such victories came at a price, however, as power vacuums among wounded and destabilized cartels led to unprecedented levels of cartel violence, with frequent bloody attacks both on government forces and on rival factions. It has been estimated that by the end of Calderón's six-year reign more than 120,000 drug-related murders had occurred within Mexico.

During this period, the Sinaloa cartel reached the peak of its power. By 2010, in spite of Calderón's public proclamations that Mexico's organized drug trade could be wiped out by military means, the Sinaloa had used bribery, blackmail and threats of violence to infiltrate both the federal government and the armed forces. Indeed, there were claims

WANTED
BY THE FBI

ASSAULTING A FEDERAL OFFICER; CONSPIRACY AND POSSESSION WITH INTENT
TO DISTRIBUTE MARIJUANA; AIDING AND ABETTING

OSIEL CARDENAS-GUILLEN

FBI No.399566A2

Photograph taken July 6, 1997   Date of Photograph Unknown

Aliases: Osiel Cardenas-Guillen, Osiel Cardenas-Gillen, "El Cabezon," "El Loco," "El Patron," "Madrina," and "Memo"

DESCRIPTION

Date of Birth:	May 18, 1967	Hair:	Brown
Place of Birth:	Mexico	Eyes:	Brown
Height:	5'9"	Complexion:	Medium
Weight:	180 lbs.	Sex:	Male
Build:	Medium	Social Security	
Occupation(s):	Unknown	Number:	N/A
Scar and Mark:	Possible tattoo on left shoulder	Race:	Hispanic
Remarks:	Subject travels with an armed security detail and is known for his tendency for violence.	Nationality:	Mexican
		NCIC:	N/A

CRIMINAL RECORD

November 5, 1992 - Possession with Intent to Distribute Cocaine

CAUTION

SHOULD BE CONSIDERED ARMED AND DANGEROUS.

A Federal warrant was issued on March 15, 2000, at Brownsville, Texas, charging OSIEL CARDENAS-GUILLEN in violation of Title 18, United States Code, Section 111, Assaulting, Resisting, or Impeding a Sworn Customs Officer; Title 18, United States Code, Section 105, Assaulting a Federal Officer (FBI Special Agent and DEA Special Agent); Title 21, United States Code, Sections 846, 841 (a) (1), and 841 (b) (1) (B), Conspiracy to Distribute Marijuana and Possession of Marijuana with Intent to Distribute; and Title 18, United States Code, Section 2 Aiding and Abetting.

IF YOU HAVE ANY INFORMATION CONCERNING THIS PERSON, PLEASE CONTACT YOUR LOCAL FBI OFFICE OR THE NEAREST U.S. EMBASSY OR CONSULATE. THE TELEPHONE NUMBERS AND ADDRESSES OF ALL FBI OFFICES ARE LISTED ON THE BACK.

REWARD

A reward of up to $2 million may be paid for information leading to the arrest or conviction of Osiel Cardenas-Guillen.

www.fbi.gov

ENTERED NCIC
Wanted Flyer 621

Wanted by the FBI: the power vacuum that followed the arrest of Gulf cartel leader Osiel Cárdenas Guillén gave El Chapo a business opportunity. It also led to a massive loss of life.

made within the Mexican and US media that the government itself and the Sinaloa were in collusion, their aim being to wipe out rival cartels, leaving Guzmán effectively under state protection and in control of the whole of Mexico's drug routes – apparently, they were hoping to bring an end to the uncontrolled spiral of violence.

At the same time, a US *Newsweek* investigation reported that Guzmán had been able to maintain his position as Mexico's dominant drugs lord by covertly providing information to the US authorities on his enemies in the Juárez cartel, and had even betrayed figures within his own organization to American agents, resulting in a large number of arrests. This goes some way to explaining how such a high-profile wanted criminal could evade the law for so long – even when he was incarcerated, he was, initially, at least, able to live a life of relative luxury behind bars.

The extent to which the cartels managed to integrate themselves within Mexico's military was particularly striking. A 2010 US Army intelligence report suggested a startling statistic, that over a six-year period 150,000 Mexican soldiers – 60 per cent of the army's total numbers – had abandoned the military to work within the drug industry.

At this time, Los Zetas, notorious as the most brutal of Mexico's drug syndicates, publicly split from the Gulf cartel, leading to the outbreak of a bloody turf war for control of the drug trade routes in north-eastern Mexico. Los Zetas themselves had originated from within the ranks of elite Mexican army commandos who had deserted to become, in effect, the military wing of the Gulf cartel. Weakened substantially by the incarceration of leader Osiel Cárdenas Guillén in 2003 – and his subsequent extradition to the United States four years later – as well as by the growing power of Los Zetas, who were now working, if only temporarily, with the Sinaloa syndicate, the Gulf unsuccessfully attempted to curtail their influence.

President Calderón's successor, Enrique Peña Nieto, came to power in 2012 on a ticket of reducing violence on the streets of Mexico, and to this he gave higher priority than direct confrontation with the drug cartels. His avowed intention was to cut murder rates by half and reduce extortion and the number of drug-related kidnappings. He gave responsibility for public security to Mexico's Interior Ministry, which was to create a new 40,000-strong 'gendarmerie' to take on these crimes. In spite of this intent, the first 14 months of his administration still saw 23,640 drug-related murders across the country.

GIVE PEACE A CHANCE

In 2018, the centre-left National Regeneration Movement party came to power in Mexico under the leadership of President Andrés Manuel López Obrador. Within a month of taking over the reins, on January 30, 2019, he declared an end to Mexico's war on drugs.

His campaign had revolved around a supposed 'strategy of peace', in which the violence would end by offering Mexicans working within the drugs industry an amnesty from prosecution. With cartel-related violence still shockingly rife, it remained hard to see precisely how this could be made to work, even if he made clear that he believed there was a definite distinction to be made between the poor rural farmers who struggled to make ends meet without the drugs trade and the gun-toting killers within the cartels.

Obrador was the first president to publicly air what many saw as the country's core problem and major impediment to defeating the drug cartels: Mexico's extraordinary social disparity.

During the first decade of the 21st century, poverty levels rose in Mexico to the point where by 2010, 46 per cent of the population (52 million people) were deemed even by government statistics to be living in 'moderate or extreme poverty'.

Fond of the rhyming soundbite, Obrador' claimed that his policy was all about *abrazos, no balazos* ('hugs, not bullets'). He regarded education as one of the most significant keys to prevent the lower classes being lured into the 'easy money' of the drugs cartels – *becarios, sí, sicarios no* ('scholarships, yes; contract killings, no').This is no easy task in a country where rural illiteracy is still a major problem; among the indigenous peoples in the south of Mexico, children still frequently get less than three years of formal schooling in total; even the national average is barely eight years compared to twelve in the United States.

Alongside a struggle to improve education, however, was the understanding that if there were not jobs and improved wages for the young – especially those living in rural areas – they would continue to be drawn to working for the drug cartels.

During international trade discussions, Obrador declared: 'Wages in our country are very low – they are the lowest wages in the world – and we need to strengthen the domestic market.This is to improve the income of workers; you cannot be paying the workers of the *maquilas* [factories that assemble duty-free items for export] 800 pesos [$40/£32] a week.'

Many of the fledgling president's statements were treated with scepticism by both his political opponents and the national media. And, as things stand, there seems to have been little radical change for Mexico's most deprived citizens.

Meanwhile, regardless of changes in leadership and shifts in power, the Mexican drug cartels continue to function much as they always did, still producing nearly all of the world's cocaine trade, becoming a growing global influence in the production of opioids such as fentanyl – a drug up to one hundred times more powerful than heroin – and acting as a gateway into the United States for almost all other illegal narcotics.

Even with El Chapo Guzmán locked away at ADX Florence, one of America's 'supermax' prisons – built to cope with prisoners too dangerous even for high-security incarceration – the Sinaloa and its rival cartels remain billion-dollar businesses.They have also grown in number. Although the fortunes of individual syndicates may fluctuate, there are currently thought to be around 37 major drug cartels currently active in Mexico. Apart from the brief period when Donald Trump launched his presidential election pledge to build a wall along America's southern border, mention of Mexico in the global media has invariably centred on the drugs trade and related violence.

Former president Calderón's aggressive use of his armed forces against the cartels from 2006 saw a clear escalation of the violence on both sides; and yet the 'softer' approach of the two administrations that followed still seems to have had a very limited impact. Indeed, according to Mexico's National Statistics Institute, 2018 saw the recording of a further 35,964 homicides.

It is this dichotomy that has faced Mexico's politicians now for more than 30 years. Traditionalists continue to believe that, regardless of past failures, the state should continue waging war on the cartels.

To many, however, this is a counter-productive strategy that masks a deeper problem. For a nation hugely rich in natural resources, Mexico is home to some of the poorest people in the world. As long as poverty, social disparity and widespread official corruption remain rife, the drug cartels, they claim, will continue to play a highly visible role in Mexican life.

Javier Valdez Cardenás, one of Mexico's leading investigative journalists on cartel-related crime, shared his own fears and hopes for the future of his country in March 2017. 'Inside me there is a pessimistic bastard, distressed and sometimes sullen, who feels like a somewhat bitter old man with watery eyes, who is bothered by having his solitude spoiled. But he dreams. I have an idea of another country, for my family and other Mexicans, that does not continue to fall into an abyss from which there may be no return.'

Two months later, a few short blocks away from the office where he worked in the city of Culiacán, Valdez was dragged from his car and shot dead. He had displeased the Sinaloa cartel.

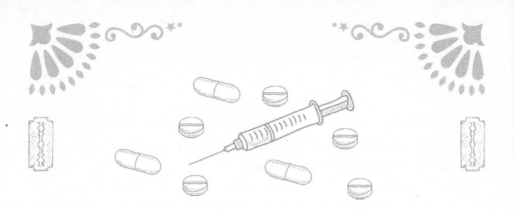

CHAPTER 2:
ORANGES AND POPPY FIELDS

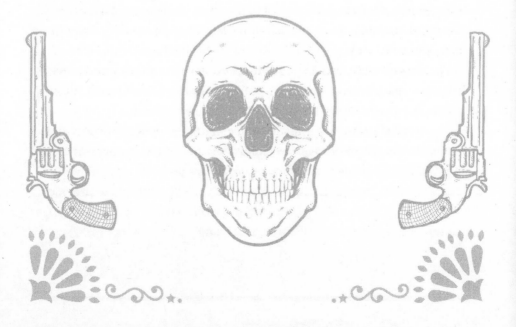

The Sierra Madre mountains run through north-western Mexico along the Gulf of California. They form part of the North American Corderilla, an almost continuous chain of mountain ranges that extends south from Alaska, passing through the Yukon, the Rockies and the Sierra Nevada, before cascading across the border into Mexico; it seems somehow fitting that what geologists refer to as the 'backbone' of North, Central and South America should also be home to Mexico's own 'Golden Triangle', an area within the Sierra Madre which has played a central role in the flow of illegal drugs into the United States for more than 40 years.

The corners of this equilateral *triangulo dorado* extend across three state boundaries, from Sinaloa in the west on the coast of the Gulf of California, to Durango in the east and Chihuahua in the north.

The terrain of the Sierra Madre is harsh; the inhabitants of its rural mountain towns and villages are among the poorest in Mexico. And its single-track dirt roads make it all but impenetrable to the outside world. The steep hills around the tiny hamlet of La Tuna de Badiraguato provide a picturesque vista in season, the bright red bulbs of the opium poppies on the highest terrain visible for miles around.

In almost every way, La Tuna in the mid-1950s was no different from any other settlement in the region. Life for its residents was one of perpetual hardship. The few hundred who lived there were crammed into a dozen or so tiny single-storey houses, each one divided into no more than two or three rooms. The buildings and facilities were basic, constructed using 'adobe' mud bricks, the floors just the earth on which they were erected. There was no sewage, electricity or running water. And anyone in need of urgent medical attention faced a severe problem; the nearest hospital was in Culiacán, more than 250 miles (400 km) away. Unsurprisingly, life expectancy barely extended beyond 40 years. Few who were born in La Tuna ever left the hamlet; most came from families who had lived there for many generations.

'They were difficult times,' recalled María Consuelo Loera Pérez in 2018. 'We longed for something better.' In the summer of 1956, María became an expectant mother for the seventh time. She and her husband Emilio Guzmán Bustillos already had two daughters, Armida and Bernarda, and four sons, Miguel Ángel, Aureliano, Arturo and Emilio; on 4 April 1957, they were joined by Joaquín Archivaldo Guzmán Loera.

With the nearest school more than 50 miles (80 km) away, educational opportunities were limited for the Guzmán family. The only formal schooling their children received was from visiting *voluntaria* teachers, often students or members of the church, who would live in the area for a matter of months before moving on to another region. Joaquín would have received little education at all beyond the age of 11; like all young males, he would be expected to start earning for the family as soon as he was deemed sufficiently strong.

In the years following World War II, the local economy still revolved mainly around cattle, farming and fruit, more often than not oranges and tomatoes. Emilio Guzmán was officially a cattle rancher, but by the time Joaquín was born he had begun to find alternative ways of supporting his wife, children and parents – as a *gummer* or *gomero*, an opium poppy farmer, and by cultivating and selling marijuana.

Lorena García watches a news report about El Chapo in the village of El Verano in the Sierra Madre, 13 January 2016. Searching for Guzmán, Mexican helicopters had opened fire on El Verano back in October 2015, terrifying villagers and sending them diving for cover. Most of the people in these parts saw El Chapo as a hero.

The start of the 1960s saw a huge surge in demand for heroin and marijuana in the United States, one that far outweighed supply; the opium poppy was found in abundance at the highest altitudes of the Sierra Madre. There the buds were scraped to provide the gum used in the production of heroin. It was backbreaking work and the hours were long.

During the harvest season, at the break of dawn, Emilio and his eldest sons would begin their daily hike from La Tuna to the opium patches high up the mountainside where the plants were best able to thrive. This was now the family business. Emilio would negotiate a selling price and the opium gum would be sold on through a chain of middlemen until it reached suppliers in the cities on the coastline – Culiacán, Guamúchil or Los Mochis. From there, it would be trafficked into the United States.

KICKED OUT

As a young boy Joaquín, small and stocky for his age, became known affectionately as 'Chapo', a common enough nickname in Hispanic countries which translates roughly as 'Shorty' – even as a fully grown adult, Guzmán peaked at 5 ft 6 in (1.68 m) in height.

As a child, Joaquín was already beginning to exhibit the ambition and determination that would one day enable him to leave behind this background of rural poverty. Each day, his mother recalled, he would haul sacks of oranges across the hills to sell for a few pesos to peasant farmers, which helped to keep his family fed. 'He always fought for a better life,' she told reporters in 2018, 'even as a small boy.'

It was a relentlessly tough childhood, as Joaquín would relate to colleagues and fellow prison inmates on more than one occasion. Emilio Guzmán was evidently a violent man who was not only prone to striking his children but would also frequently squander the family's meagre earnings on alcohol and prostitutes. Joaquín's relationship with his father eventually broke down when he had to step in to prevent his younger siblings from receiving beatings.

Kicked out of the family home, Joaquín moved in with his grandfather. It was Emilio, though, who gave Joaquín his first taste of the narcotics industry; by the time he was 12, he had joined his brothers working in the family business on the opium fields.

A smart mind for business ensured that he quickly tired of his father's haphazard ways of doing things, and at the age of 15 he began cultivating a marijuana plantation of his own with four of his cousins. On a video Guzmán posted in January 2016, just a few days before his final arrest, he confirmed: 'There [were] no job opportunities, [the way] to be able to buy food was to grow poppy and marijuana, and from that age I began to grow it, to harvest it, to sell it… Drug trafficking is already part of a culture that originated from the ancestors.'

He was quite right in that Sinaloa had been home to Mexico's first drug-smugglers. And in the past the Sierra Madre mountains had often proved attractive to criminals. On the run from both American and Mexican forces in the early 20th century, the revolutionary leader Pancho Villa was able to hide himself away in the foothills of Chihuahua.

And long before El Chapo's own celebrity, Sinaloa had long mythologized the bandit Jesús Malverde, the 'Mexican Robin Hood', so much so that he is still remembered annually in Culiacán more than a century after his hanging.

Each year on 3 May, followers gather at his shrine with gifts of cigarettes and whisky, the large bust of Malverde is loaded on to the bonnet of a truck and the 'Narco Saint' is paraded through the city. In fact, there is scant evidence that Malverde ever actually existed, but he remains a powerful symbolic presence and is even known as a kind of 'patron saint' to drug-smugglers – pistols, AK-47 rifles and other criminal ephemera are known to have been left at his shrine.

Modern-day violent criminals like El Chapo are also venerated by some in the region, though, and it's not hard to see why. The inhabitants are surrounded by poverty and are given little in the way of assistance by the federal government or local authorities; when the cartels step in with offers of jobs and welfare, their leaders can literally be seen as life-savers. As Professor José Luis González of Mexico's National School of Anthropology and History puts it: 'The tensions of living in crisis lead people to look for symbolic figures that can help them face danger.'

Many activities that were illegal in 1960s Mexico were socially acceptable in Sinaloa – the smuggling of clothes and food from the United States, for instance, which was then banned by the federal government – so it's unsurprising that the growth in the cultivation and trafficking of illegal narcotics would hardly pose any great moral dilemma to its citizens.

That drug culture would be able to thrive so successfully within the *triangulo dorado* was also in part down to the geography of the region: in the large, sparsely populated and impenetrable area, there was little in the way of effective government or police force. Traditionally, this was a function of nominated locals who would report back to the municipal authorities in Culiacán.

At the time of El Chapo Guzmán's birth, domestic violence and sexual abuse, invariably fuelled by alcoholism, were rife in the region. Although mothers are traditionally revered in Mexican culture by their sons – El Chapo called María Consuelo 'my foundation of emotional support' – the women of Sierra Madre were poorly treated and enjoyed little by way of protection. There was simply nobody to administer the law of the land.

Once again, organized crime was able to step into the vacuum; the drug lords provided their own sets of self-serving 'rules', helping and protecting local populations and meting out 'justice' to others. Life in Sierra Madre might have been lawless in an official sense, but order was maintained nevertheless.

NEW HORIZONS

By the middle of the 1970s, Joaquín Guzmán along with other young Sinaloans, such as his future partners – and later deadly enemies – the Beltrán Levya brothers, were making a living from their marijuana plantations. But Guzmán was eager to expand his horizons.

That opportunity come from a valuable family connection. His uncle, Pedro Avilés Pérez, had been one of the pioneers of Mexican narco-crime. Known as 'El Leon de la Sierra' (the Mountain Lion), Aviles had been one of the most significant figures in the growth of the trafficking of heroin and marijuana between Sinaloa and the United States in the 1960s. He was even reputed to have been the first trafficker to have used private aircraft to smuggle cocaine brought in from Colombia across the US border. By the time Joaquín Guzmán was 20, he had escaped the confines of El Tuna and was working full-time for his uncle's organization in Culiacán.

In many respects, the Sinaloa drugs chain was shaped by President Richard M. Nixon's declaration, on 17 July 1971, that drug use was 'public enemy number one' and had now 'assumed the dimensions of a national emergency'. Initially driven less by domestic narcotics abuse than by concerns of addiction among US troops fighting in Vietnam, Nixon asked Capitol Hill for $84 million (£67m) to enable urine-testing to be implemented.

This was the beginning of what the following year would become known as the 'war on drugs', when Nixon's bill became law: 'I am convinced that the only way to fight this menace is by attacking it on many fronts.' He further described his aim of repelling 'a tide which has swept through the country in the past decade and which afflicts both the body and soul of America'. To this end, in 1973, Nixon created the Drug Enforcement Agency (DEA), a special police force committed to targeting the trafficking of drugs into the United States.

(Decades later, Nixon's assistant for Domestic Affairs, John Ehrlichman, claimed that the war on drugs had been created in part to smear the groups the President saw as his opponents. The Nixon Whitehouse had two enemies, he declared, 'The anti-war left and black people... We knew we couldn't make it illegal to be either against the war or blacks, but by getting the public to associate the hippies with marijuana and blacks with heroin, and then criminalizing both heavily, we could disrupt those communities. We could arrest their leaders, raid their homes, break up their meetings, and vilify them night after night on the evening news.')

In 1975, the DEA, in conjunction with the Mexican government, began Operation Condor, a crop-eradication programme aimed at wiping out the fields of poppies used in the making of heroin. This was followed a year later by Operation Trizo, which enabled Mexican nationals to fly US State Department planes and helicopters to spray herbicides on the poppy plantations of the Golden Triangle – 22,000 acres (8,900 hectares) were destroyed and 4,000 people arrested.

It quickly became clear that this would cause unprecedented economic chaos and social unrest in Sinaloa, so the Mexican government requested that the operation be halted. The United States would nevertheless declare it a major success: 'The purity of heroin fell to just five per cent, its lowest in seven years… Operation Trizo lessened demand for Mexican heroin in the US market.'

On 15 September 1978, Pedro Avilés Pérez was killed in a shoot-out with the Mexican federal police. The operation was taken over by one of his protégés, Miguel Ángel Félix Gallardo, a man who would alter the trajectory of the Mexican drugs business.

Throughout the 1980s, he reorganized the existing drug production and trafficking industry with the formation of the Guadalajara cartel, crucially forging new links with Colombia's cocaine producers and using his knowledge of local politics to corrupt officials. El Chapo Guzmán may be the most globally famous of all the narco-barons, but Miguel Ángel Félix Gallardo was the founding figure of the Mexican cartels – indeed, he would be known as *El Padrino* (The Godfather), the man who created the template used to the present day by his successors.

LOW PROFILE

El Chapo Guzmán forged his early reputation within the Guadalajara cartel, handling shipments of cocaine for Héctor Luis Palma Salazar. Known as 'El Güero' (Paleface), Palma was a former car thief who rose through the ranks to become one of Félix Gallardo's right-hand men.

Guzmán's job was overseeing the air transportation of drugs from Sierra Madre to the US-Mexican border. El Chapo had married 19-year-old Alejandrina María Salazar Hernández in 1977 and they were now living 60 miles (96 km) outside Culiacán on a ranch in the town of Jesús Maria. Together they would have three children, Iván Archivaldo, Jesús Alfredo and César. (The little-known César seems to have enjoyed a successful commercial career in his own right, although there remain conflicting reports about his fate; American tabloid the *New York Post* reported that he was killed in 2012.) Iván Archivaldo and Jesús Alfredo would, on the other hand, follow their father into the family business.

Guzmán had not yet developed his infamous taste for ostentation and seems to have kept a low profile during this time, socializing little and

Drug lord Héctor Luis Palma Salazar, one of the founders of the Sinaloa cartel, is escorted by masked Mexican marines on arrival back in his home country after serving almost a decade in a US jail. He looks a broken man.

devoting most of his energy to his work. Ambitious from the outset, he persistently pushed his superiors for more responsibility and asked them to allow him to shift ever larger amounts of product.

But there were other stories emerging around Culiacán of a fearsome new figure: traffickers trying to cheat him or sell his goods to a competitor, or incompetent subordinates, were all liable to be found with a bullet through the head.

This short guy went about his business calmly, efficiently and ruthlessly. It was a modus operandi approved by his superiors and soon El Chapo Guzmán came to the notice of Félix Gallardo. The DEA meanwhile had turned its attention to the Colombian cocaine supply chain that stretched all the way to Florida. It was supplied by Pablo Escobar's Medellín cartel.

As the supply routes were investigated and closed down one by one, the Colombians needed a new method of getting large amounts of their product into the United States. Crossing the Mexican border was the only option.

Eventually, in 1982, after an 18-month undercover sting, the DEA's Operation Swordfish more or less rendered the Miami route unusable. In the eyes of the Medellín and Cali cartels, their Mexican middlemen were becoming increasingly important.

Miguel Ángel Félix Gallardo was born in 1946 at his family's ranch in Bellavista, a small town on the outskirts of Culiacán. He received a considerably broader education than most of his compatriots, graduating from high school and going on to college as a business student. His first job was with the federal police; he left in his mid-20s to take on a security position with the governor of Sinaloa, Leopoldo Sánchez Celis.

With direct links to some of the most powerful officials in the region, and a growing knowledge of the way these powers bases operated, Gallardo had become by the mid-1970s one of Pedro Avilés Pérez's key lieutenants. With poppy production decimated by Operation Trizo, Avilés and Gallardo used their marijuana- and heroin-trafficking networks to take cocaine across the border.

Following the death of Avilés, Gallardo along with his two lieutenants, Rafael Caro Quintero and Ernesto Fonseca Carrillo, modernized and commercialized their predecessor's organization. El Padrino would also create important international networks; routes established between Mexico, the United States, South America, Europe and Asia remain in use to the present day.

Through the trafficker Juan Matta-Ballesteros, Gallardo was able to connect directly with Pablo Escobar's Medellín cartel, creating the first significant business links between the Colombian and Mexican drugs cartels. Revenue would be laundered into the legal economy – something that Guzmán himself would later perfect – as armies of individuals were hired to deposit amounts lower than $10,000 (£8,000) which would avoid detection by the US banks. In other cases, trade-based laundering saw revenue spent on buying electronics items in the

US which could be taken back across the border and sold 'legitimately' for pesos in Mexico.

Above all, it was El Padrino's skill in rooting out government officials and members of the police and military who could be 'bought' that would eventually make it possible for the cartels to achieve such power and influence within Mexico.

By some accounts – including the CIA's – he even enjoyed the protection of Mexico's Federal Security Directorate (DFS). The Guadalajara cartel, as it became known, became the dominant force in the region. They staged an uneasy 'truce' with the Mexican government and other criminal organizations, a kind of *Pax Mafiosa*, that guaranteed stability so long as everyone stuck to their own territories and did not interfere in the business of others.

STUCK IN THE MIDDLE

At this stage, in the early 1980s, the Mexicans were still little more than the middlemen in the process. The two major Colombian cartels – the Medellín and the Cali – would ship their products to Mexico where El Padrino and his cohorts would be paid to move them across the 2,000-mile (3,200-km) border. This was a difficult job involving thousands of trucks making daily journeys through the 50 or so border crossings. In 1981, having impressed Gallardo with his handling of shipments of cocaine in Sierra Madre, El Chapo Guzmán was handed his first sizeable promotion – responsibility for cartel logistics. That he was successful can be illustrated by a single statistic: in 1982, cocaine – now being trafficked into the US almost exclusively by the Mexicans – had surpassed coffee as Colombia's chief export.

As the Guadalajara cartel grew in power and influence, so did El Chapo Guzmán's own position as he and his associate, Ismael 'El Mayo' Zambada García, began to collect 'connections' within the government of Sinaloa – among them, the governor himself. Guzmán began to develop an appetite not only for the high life, but also for women.

Much of El Chapo's early personal life is shrouded in mystery, making it hard to pin down the truth of what happened. We don't know precisely how many times he's been married or how many children he has fathered.

One story has it that while still married to Alejandrina, Guzmán fell for a young bank clerk named Estela Peña; after having his advances rebuffed on a number of occasions, Guzmán kidnapped and raped her. Then, it seems, they were married. Many are sceptical, but the sequence of events has been published in some parts of the press who regard Estela Peña as Guzmán's second wife.

What is certain is that by the middle of the 1980s he was married once again, this time to Griselda López Pérez, with whom he would have four children, Edgar, Joaquín, Ovidio and Griselda Guadalupe. There have even been suggestions that Guzmán's marriages overlapped. At his trial in 2018, his defence successfully objected to questions about his marital status. As one of his attorneys, William Purpura, told the judge: 'The fact that he might have three other wives at the same time he was married to Griselda, there's no relevance to that.'

As the decade played out, the inauguration in 1981 of President Ronald Reagan would have an increasing impact on the balance of power within Mexico's drug organizations.

Reagan held extremely conservative views and took a strong anti-drug stance, quickly turning his attention to the cocaine that seemed to be flowing so freely into the United States. The main target was Pablo Escobar and the Medellín cartel, both of whom had been vilified by the Colombian and US governments, but at the same time DEA undercover agents were looking for a way into the Guadalajara cartel as the major trafficker of narcotics into the United States.

Thirty-seven-year-old Enrique 'Kiki' Camarena was one of a number of DEA agents based in the city. An agent with more than ten years' experience, Camarena managed to infiltrate the highest levels of the cartel, including, it was said, meeting with El Padrino Gallardo himself.

In 1984, information gathered by Camarena resulted in a prolonged government attack on a marijuana plantation in Allende in the northern part of the Golden Triangle. Rancho Búfalo covered 2,500 acres (1010 hectares) – equivalent to almost 2,000 American football fields – employed around 10,000 farmers and produced an estimated annual crop worth $8 billion (£6.3bn).

The operation featured 450 Mexican troops backed by military helicopters; the plantation was razed. The cartel realized that the detailed information had come from the inside; Camarena was an immediate suspect.

On 7 February 1985, Camarena left the office to meet his wife for lunch. She would never see him alive again. At El Chapo's trial in 2018, a former policeman, Rene López Romero, who had become a bodyguard for Gallardo's lieutenant Rafael Caro Quintero, testified in court, describing the abduction in vivid, gruesome detail. An employee of the American consulate had pointed Camarena out to one of the kidnappers who accosted him, showed him a gun and bundled him into a waiting car.

Blindfolded, he was driven to 881 Lope de Vega, one of the cartel's Guadalajara residences. He was embraced by Caro, who declared: 'I told you I was going to have you in my hands, you son of a bitch.' Camarena was subjected to 30 hours of brutal torture, his body pummelled and burned with cigarettes. Damningly, López also claimed that high-ranking political and law-enforcement figures were present in the house – defence minister Juan Arévalo Gardoqui, interior minister Manuel Bartlett Diaz, Jalisco governor Enrique Álvarez del Castillo, Mexican federal judicial police director Manuel Ibarra Herrera and Mexican Interpol director Miguel Aldana Ibarra – and that the abduction had apparently taken place with their approval. Unsurprisingly, the allegations were strenuously denied by all.

The kidnapping caused outrage within the DEA as well as inter-agency conflict as suspicions arose that CIA agents had been involved

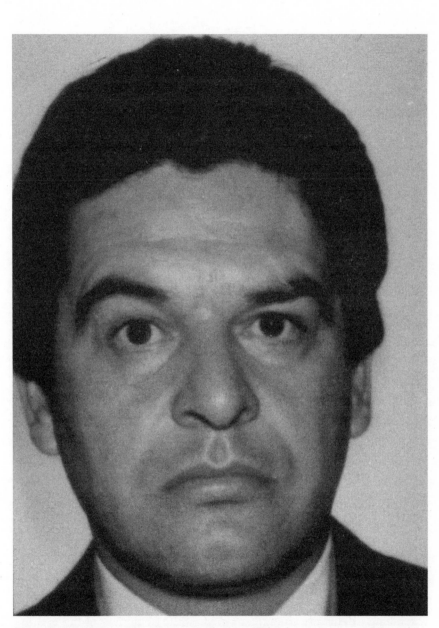

Mexican-American undercover agent Enrique 'Kiki' Camarena was abducted, then tortured and murdered by the Sinaloa. The DEA came back at the cartels with Operation Leyenda.

in the abduction, viewing Camarena as politically expendable while they conducted covert drugs-for-arms deals with South American rebel groups, a claim that is still widely believed – and denied – to the present day.

The DEA responded with the launch of Operation Leyenda (Operation Legend), still the agency's biggest-ever homicide investigation, despatching a special unit to Guadalajara. There they soon established Miguel Ángel Félix Gallardo, Rafael Caro Quintero and Ernesto Fonseca Carrillo as the main suspects behind the kidnapping.

The investigation eventually led to a field on the outskirts of the town of La Angostura, 75 miles (120 km) away in the state of Michoacán. There they unearthed two corpses wrapped in plastic, Camarena and Alfredo Zavala Avelara, a Mexican pilot used by the DEA who had disappeared the same day. Camarena's ribs had been crushed and a metal object had penetrated his skull.

The news rocked the Reagan Administration, which demanded swift action from the Mexican government, and both Caro and Fonseca were arrested.

In March 1985, Caro bribed a police chief with $300,000 (£238,000) to allow him to flee to Costa Rica in a private aircraft, but he was nonetheless recaptured a month later. The Mexican government refused US demands for extradition and both were sentenced to 40 years in prison.

Felix Gallardo still enjoyed political protection within Mexico, but he was a wanted man in the United States, and if Operation Leyenda had shown anything it was that that when pushed too hard the DEA had the power to put real pressure on the Mexican government.

BEGINNING OF THE END

The killing of Enrique Camarena signalled the beginning of the end for the Guadalajara cartel and by the end of the decade the shape of the Mexican drug-trafficking industry had changed beyond recognition. Félix

Gallardo would always maintain his innocence regarding the murder. In his prison memoirs, he wrote: 'I was taken to the DEA. I greeted them and they wanted to talk. I only answered that I had no involvement in the Camarena case and I said: "You said a madman would do it and I am not mad. I am deeply sorry for the loss of your agent."'

In 1987, Gallardo moved his family from Sinaloa to Guadalajara in an attempt to lower his profile, but he knew he was living on borrowed time. His luck finally ran out on 8 April 1989, when he opened his front door to find a 12-man police taskforce waiting for him. The Mexican president, Carlos Salinas de Gortari, had given the Americans his word that *El Padrino*, despite his protectors within the government, would be seized. Mexico's attorney general described the operation as 'clean work, without a single gunshot'.

Félix Gallardo was charged with racketeering and drug-smuggling as well as the kidnapping and murder of Enrique Camarena. Gallardo believed that he had been double-crossed by the allegedly corrupt police chief Guillermo Calderoni.

In a later interview, Calderoni described El Padrino's final moments of freedom. 'One of the agents went upstairs to get the clothes that [his] wife gave him. He was face down. I made him turn over. I put the AK-47 in his mouth and made him stand up slowly. When I took the gun away, he offered me – I can't remember whether it was $5 or $6 million [£4–4.75m] – in exchange for his release. I told him that his arrest was not negotiable – he was going to be turned over to the authorities in Mexico.'

Rumours would later persist that he had been shopped by his former protégé Joaquín Guzmán, in an ambitious power-grab. Gallardo's arrest was a sensational news story across Mexico, exposing to the public for the first time the depth of official corruption that existed in Mexico.

Within days, a number of high-ranking police commanders had been apprehended and upwards of a hundred police officers were said to have deserted – many of them to work full time for the cartels. By the time of his arrest, Gallardo was believed to have accrued assets of $500 million (£400m), including 50 houses and 200 ranches across Mexico.

Gallardo began a 40-year jail sentence in 1990 and for a while was able to live comfortably surrounded by books, still able to run cartel business from his cellphone, or through lawyers and assorted intermediaries, but it was clear that this could not last for ever.

A meeting of senior figures in the organization was convened in the southern city of Acapulco, where it was proposed that responsibilities should be divided up among his lieutenants based on their existing trading routes. Smaller self-sufficient units, Gallardo argued from his prison cell, would be less visible to the authorities and more difficult to target en masse. The route along the northwest coast that moved product into San Diego and southern California was handed to the Arellano Félix brothers, Benjamín and Ramón; the Tijuana cartel, as it would become known, soon established a reputation for its violent and intimidating operating methods.

The important route on the border sprawl that encompassed Ciudad Juárez in Mexico and El Paso, Texas would be run by the Carillo Fuentes family, headed by Amado Carillo, the nephew of Ernesto Fonseca Carrillo; this would become the Juárez cartel. The Sonora corridor in the North West bordering Arizona in the United States was handed to Miguel Caro Quintero, Rafael's brother.

On the eastern coast, Juan García Abrego was already largely an independent operator who could be left undisturbed to run what would be known as the Gulf cartel. Meanwhile, the crucial Pacific routes would be handled by Héctor Luis Palma Salazar and Gallardo's rising young protégé, Joaquín 'El Chapo' Guzmán; initially known as the *La Alianza de Sangre* (Blood Alliance) it would become more widely recognized as the Sinaloa cartel. The key players in Mexico's drug industry had been redefined at a stroke.

Gallardo was effectively taken out of the picture in 1992. All of his former privileges were lost with his transfer to the hard-line Altiplano prison complex in Almoloya de Juárez. Former DEA agent Michael Vigil described his reaction to the move: 'The commander who transported him to the maximum-security prison told me Félix Gallardo cried the entire trip to the prison and lamented it would be the end of him. It was an accurate assumption… after incarceration there, the reign of Gallardo ended, despite his power and wealth.'

He was to remain there for more than 20 years. In December 2014, at the age of 68, federal authorities agreed that because of his age and declining health he would be allowed to move to a medium-security jail in Guadalajara.

TAKING PRECAUTIONS

With Gallardo off the scene, the leaders of Mexico's new drug groups immediately took steps to consolidate their own power bases. Using the Mafia as a model, El Chapo Guzmán surrounded himself with people he knew he would be able to trust from Sierra Madre, mostly family – brothers, cousins and nephews – or those he had known over a long period. He instructed his people to buy properties under assumed names on his behalf throughout Mexico.

Deliberately chosen to be anonymous, these were usually simple two-storey houses in residential areas of provincial towns or nondescript apartments in Mexico City. They were places that his operatives could use without attracting attention from neighbours or the authorities. They could function as hideouts or as venues to stash drugs, banknotes and weapons. Each cell was given a high degree of autonomy and operated its own ranking structure (few outside Guzmán's close circle, or his personal bodyguards, ever got to meet their boss). Their job was simple: to look after the drugs until they were instructed to move the shipment on to the next link in the chain or to guard payments until they were collected. Security was paramount.

Guzmán hired deserters from the army, in particular those with expertise in using guns, bombs and rocket-launchers. These were

El Chapo's *sicarios*, his killers, and they could be relied upon to 'remove' enemies at his behest.

At this time, El Chapo was barely known to the US authorities. His name had cropped up briefly during a court case in 1987 when a criminal-turned-witness described him as the 'boss of our organization'. Three years later, an Arizona court heard how he had trafficked cocaine into the state using a fleet of trucks with false floors and delivered the shipments to a warehouse in Tucson.

With border crossings coming under increasing scrutiny, El Chapo was forced to come up with more ingenious approaches, most famously his so-called 'drug tunnels', the first of which was built in 1989. Like Ciudad Juárez in Mexico and El Paso, Texas, Agua Prieta in the north-eastern part of Sonora state is a border town that 'merges' into Douglas, Arizona with a physical border wall dividing the two.

The tunnel's designer was an architect named Felipe de Jesús Corona-Verbera who had seemingly worked for El Chapo on many other previous building projects. One of El Chapo's associates, a lawyer from Guadalajara named Francisco Rafael Camarena, fronted the scheme, which began with him buying up industrial land alongside the border wall in Douglas where he set up a building supplies company called Douglas Redi-Mix Concrete.

A warehouse was then erected on the land barely 100 feet (30 m) from the wall. Directly opposite on the other side of the wall in Agua Prieta, Camarana bought a massive plot of land and built a luxury ranch-style home. A tunnel was then dug at 30 feet (9 m) below ground level which passed under the wall joining the two buildings on either side. Three hundred feet long (90 m), 4 feet (1.2 m) in width and 5 feet (1.5 m) in height, it was just big enough for a person to push a cart filled with cocaine undetected between Mexico and the United States.

In this instance, the Arizona police received word of suspicious activity in Douglas and raided the warehouse, uncovering 2,258 pounds (1,024 kilos) of cocaine. They also discovered a pool table on a hydraulic lift: when raised, it revealed the entrance to the tunnel. Customs agent Terry Kirkpatrick, who was there on the night of the raid was taken aback. 'This whole tunnel was something that had not been seen before,' he remarked. 'And no one, I think, in the United States government — especially in law enforcement – realized anything like this ever existed.'

The US authorities estimated that the tunnel had been used daily for at least six months before its discovery and would have cost at least $1.5 million (£1.2m) to construct. Although Francisco Rafael Camarena was able to flee the scene, he was eventually captured and extradited to the United States for trial in 2001; Felipe de Jesus Corona-Verbera denied any involvement with El Chapo Guzmán and the Sinaloa cartel, but he faced a similar fate in 2016. Both were convicted.

In spite of the bust, Guzmán declared the project a success and had many similar tunnels built – including the one that, famously, was used to help him abscond from his prison cell. Nobody knows with any certainty how many drug tunnels are in existence, but in 2015 US government statistics revealed that in the previous 25 years 181 illegal 'passages' had been discovered.

The impact of the expansion of the tunnel network was also noticed by El Chapo's Colombian business partners, who began referring to him as El Rápido (Speedy). Miguel Ángel Martínez recalled: 'If three planes arrived per week, now ten were arriving... before the planes were arriving back in Colombia on the return, the cocaine was already in Los Angeles.' He claimed that Guzmán had told him: 'Corona [Felipe de Jesús Corona-Verbera] made a fucking cool tunnel. Tell them to send all the drugs they can.'

So how was El Chapo able to get these tunnels built at such speed? According to the DEA, Mexican workers from some of the country's poorest regions had been press-ganged or lured with the promise of lucrative employment. 'They're going to grab these kids and are holding them hostage until they finish the work,' believed DEA agent Doug Coleman. 'Sometimes they pay them. Sometimes they don't.' And not all of them survived. As security, and as a deterrent to would-be complainers or informers, 'sometimes when the job was over they made them disappear'.

OFF THEIR HEADS

El Chapo had other ingenious tricks up his sleeve. In 1990, the DEA arrested José Reynoso Gonzalez, whose grocery wholesaling business was being used by Guzmán as a front to distribute Sinaloa product. In the warehouse, they discovered 1,400 cans of La Comadre brand pickled jalapeño peppers packed with over 7 tons (6,350 kg) of cocaine.

One of Guzmán's 'managers', Miguel Angel Martinez, would later describe in court how packers at the cartel's facility in Mexico City inhaled large quantities of the drug while filling the six-pound (2.7 kilo) cans. 'They got intoxicated because whenever you pressed the kilos, it would release cocaine into the air,' he laughed. The La Comadre cans would be filled with a half-kilo (1.1 lb) of cocaine and then topped up with sand so that they achieved the correct weight. Trucks would carry up to 3,000 cans at a time, mixed in with cans of genuine peppers. He estimated that up to $500 million (£396m) worth of cocaine reached Los Angeles each year in this way.

The DEA realized that in El Chapo Guzmán it was up against a smart and well-organized adversary. Anything that could be used to conceal shipments of cocaine, heroin and marijuana was fair game: freight trains carrying cooking oil, chicken wire with compartments – it was even suggested that Mexico's state petrochemical company, Pemex, had discussed with El Chapo the idea of transporting cocaine in their tankers.

These clever innovations doubtless modernized the way the drug industry operated, but although unafraid to use the most brutal violence when he saw fit, Guzmán also took lessons from his mentor, El Padrino, who taught him the value of creating alliances, getting to know the right people in positions of power… and establishing early on those who could be 'bought'.

It was said that on one occasion in 1991, Guzmán was arrested in Mexico City; he asked to see the chief of police, handed him a suitcase containing $50,000 (£39,000) and was allowed to walk from the station a free man. Similarly, he was reported to have bribed a chief of police in Jalisco with $1 million (£800,000) and five Dodge Ram Charger SUVs to allow two aircraft to land and unload their cargo of cocaine.

The start of the 1990s saw a gradual shift in the balance of power between the Colombian suppliers and the Mexican distributors. El Chapo's lieutenant, Miguel Angel Martinez, reported that 55 per cent of the proceeds from each transaction would go to the Colombian suppliers, the remainder belonging to El Chapo and the Sinaloa cartel. As the US-supported Colombian government began to take action against the Medellín and Cali cartels, drug lords like El Chapo and the Arellano Félix brothers set about negotiating improved deals. They were rich in cash, but instead of being paid to traffic product by the Colombians they would now buy and sell the cocaine themselves. The new profit margins were astronomical.

Of course, central to Gallardo's intent behind splitting up the Guadalajara cartel was that each organization would have its own well-defined *plaza*, the 'turf' on which it was allowed to conduct its business. It would be possible to maintain order only as long as the new cartels respected these boundaries. El Chapo Guzmán was an ambitious man who had already begun to forge strategic alliances. His sights were set on the lucrative trafficking routes from the Baja California peninsula through to San Diego which belonged to the Tijuana cartel. There could be only one outcome: war.

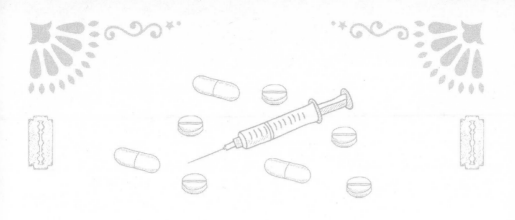

CHAPTER 3:
THE FIGHT
FOR TIJUANA

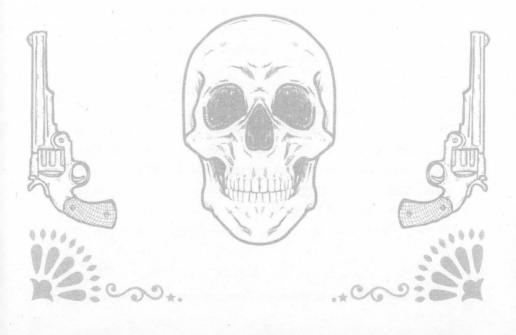

The incarcerated Miguel Ángel Félix Gallardo believed that by splitting up his Guadalajara cartel by regions and routes he could protect the interests of everyone engaged in trafficking narcotics between Mexico and the United States. Yet conflict escalated almost from the outset.

The San Diego-Tijuana transborder conurbation was strategically crucial to the Colombians for trafficking cocaine between Mexico and California. And this meant that it was prized by the cartels. El Chapo Guzmán made an immediate strategic move on the *plaza*, which, unsurprisingly, the Arellano Félix brothers' Tijuana group considered a serious encroachment.

The brothers had already carved out a brutal reputation among Mexico's criminal organizations, but El Chapo, his partner Héctor Luis Palma Salazar, and associate El Mayo Zambada were ready and willing to take them on. Guzmán had already infuriated his rivals by building his infamous cross-border tunnel on their patch. He had also started to acquire properties in the city to store firearms and cash. He was now a prime target for the Arellano Félix clan.

Hostilities broke out in 1989, when one of El Chapo's closest colleagues,

Armando Lopez, was murdered. Like many other cartel-related tales, there are several accounts as to what actually happened, as well as more fanciful scenarios found in TV narco-dramas.

Whether he was deliberately sent to Tijuana by Guzmán to negotiate with the Arellano Félixes or – as some accounts would have it – he had drunkenly attempted to crash one of their parties, Lopez was shot in the head by one of the brothers, Ramón Arellano Félix. The body was dumped unceremoniously on the outskirts of the city and, to avoid reprisals, a hit squad was sent to execute members of Lopez's family.

In January 1992, the Arellano Félixes made a co-ordinated statement of intent. One of their hit squads, the San Diego-based Logan Heights gang, also known as Calle Treinta, captured six of El Chapo's men in Tijuana. They were tortured for information, executed and their bodies bound, gagged and dumped on the highway. And then a car bomb went off outside a house known to be used by El Chapo in Sinaloa. On that occasion, the building was empty.

The Sinaloa struck back on 3 September with an attack that saw nine dead, among them lawyers and the family of Félix Gallardo. The Attorney General ordered an investigation into the killings, but this was quickly abandoned; years later, it would be discovered that El Chapo had paid officials 10 million pesos ($445,000/£353,000) to call off the enquiry.

NARROW ESCAPE

In November 1992, Guzmán had his closest shave to date when Ramón Arellano Félix and four of his *sicarios* waited for him as his car passed through the streets of Guadalajara. A burst from AK-47 rifles holed the vehicle, but driver and passengers escaped unharmed.

The attack was enough to convince Guzmán that Guadalajara was no longer the safe haven it had once been. He had long convinced himself that the key to avoiding being caught by the authorities – and now being eliminated by rivals – was to remain unpredictable and always to be on the move. On top of that, he always tried to travel around with a large entourage of discreetly armed men.

When journeying away from home turf he would take rooms in multiple hotels and make a spur-of-the-moment decision as to where he would stay. He would sometimes disguise himself too, donning the uniform of a priest, military officer or other high-status figure, and in this way he was confident his travels could pass uninterrupted.

Days after the attack on his car, El Chapo escalated hostilities. On 8 November 1992, 15 Sinaloa gunmen wearing federal police uniforms stormed Christine's, a nightclub in the beach resort of Puerto Vallarta known to be a regular haunt of the Arellano Félix brothers.

Among the crowd of 300 partying on the dance floor, they spied Ramón and Francisco Javier, as well as their security chief David Barron Corona. They opened fire. More than a thousand rounds were unleashed during eight minutes of pandemonium. Six innocent bystanders were killed and dozens wounded. The brothers meanwhile escaped through an air-conditioning duct in the rest room and sped away in a waiting car.

While the two groups engaged in an increasingly violent, yet ultimately fruitless, procession of tit-for-tat actions, on the other side of the country Juan García Abrego's Gulf cartel took advantage of the situation in Baja California. They could guarantee the Medellín and Cali cartels that their product would make its way pretty well unhindered between the drop-off points along the east coast trafficking routes. They had infiltrated key departments in the Mexican navy and bribed officers to turn a blind eye to the sudden increase in air traffic coming in from Colombia to local airstrips.

GET SHORTY

The conflict between the Sinaloa and Tijuana cartels had thus far been viewed by the authorities as a local dispute. In May 1993, it turned into an international news story. In the six months since the Christine's nightclub massacre, the Arellano Félix brothers had made it clear there could now be only one outcome: as a matter of urgency, El Chapo must be removed.

Francisco Javier Arellano Félix, accompanied by his crack Logan Heights hit squad, headed out to Guadalajara to kill Guzmán. The Sinaloa leader was well protected in the city, though, and after a week of following fruitless leads they decided to head back to their home turf of Baja California.

On 24 May as Francisco Javier waited at Guadalajara International Airport to book his return flight, he received word from David Barron Corona that El Chapo Guzmán and his personal bodyguards were *at that very moment* in the airport carpark outside the building. Barron Corona's intelligence suggested that Guzmán was waiting in a white Mercury Grand Marquis, a car he was known to have used – and a popular choice among narco bosses. The door was wrenched open and round after round was fired at the driver and passenger.

August 2006: Francisco Javier Arellano Félix is taken off a US Coast Guard vessel and removed to a waiting DEA SUV. He was apprehended in a fishing boat off the coast of Baja California.

In the chaotic scenes that followed, the carpark turned into a hellish war zone, with the Tijuana and Sinaloa gunmen slugging away at one another. Later, it turned out that Guzmán had, in fact, been in the airport carpark but was in the passenger seat of a dark green Buick Sedan; amid the mayhem, he crept out of the car, jumped into a taxi and headed for a Sinaloa safe house in Bugambilias, a 20-minute drive from the airport. Meanwhile, Arellano Félix boarded his flight as planned and returned to Tijuana; by the time the police arrived, the gunmen – numbering 20 according to news reports – had already dispersed.

Then came the news that was to cause shock and outrage across all of Mexico. In the white Mercury lay the bullet-riddled bodies of Cardinal Juan Jesús Posadas Ocampo and his chauffeur. Five others were killed during the shoot-out.

The 66-year-old cardinal was well-known in Mexico and a senior figure within the Catholic Church. Significantly, he was also publicly outspoken

The bodies of two of the victims from the shoot-out at Guadalajara airport. Cardinal Juan Jesús Posadas Ocampo also died in the incident.

on the evils of the drugs trade and had called upon the government to take a strong stance against the trafficking organizations.

The horrifying execution made headline news across the world. President Carlos Salinas de Gortari condemned the shooting as 'a criminal act that targeted innocent civilians' and flew to Guadalajara to show his support. Francisco Corona Garcia of the Attorney General's office gave his initial thoughts on the identities of the gunmen. 'It appears that they were drug-traffickers,' he claimed. And this would remain the official line: that Cardinal Posadas Ocampo had been the unfortunate victim of a mistaken identity.

Yet there were clearly questions that needed to be asked. How would it be possible to confuse the short, stocky 36-year-old Guzmán with a taller man almost twice his age who was wearing a black cassock and large crucifix? Was this a revenge attack on a public figure who had taken a stand against the cartels? After two years of an official enquiry, the government concluded that the cardinal had indeed been murdered by mistake. The majority of the Mexican public, not to mention the Catholic Church, believed otherwise.

'We do not agree with that hypothesis,' the Cardinal's successor, Cardinal Juan Sandoval Íñiguez, declared. 'We have never believed in the idea of a confusion, and we hope they will someday solve the case.'

A CAN OF WORMS

The case would be reopened in 2000 after the election of President Vicente Fox, who vowed to clear up a number of high-profile murders inherited from past regimes. Serious irregularities with the original investigation were cited, including police obstruction and thousands of missing official documents. Testimonies claimed that Cardinal Posadas Ocampo had been threatened by then-president Carlos Solinas in person, leading to the theory that his murder may have been sanctioned by the government because he possessed information linking high-ranking politicians to the drug trade.

Popular TV shows like the Netflix series *El Chapo* may have taken this more dramatically appealing storyline, but no such official conclusions were ever reached. In a country where corruption within government, police and military has seemed almost de rigueur in the past, the murder of Cardinal Posadas Ocampo remains a contentious issue.

As a controversial postscript to the story, it was later revealed that through an intermediary priest, who also happened to be a 'family friend', Ramón and Benjamín Arellano Félix had met secretly in December 1993, and again a month later, with Girolamo Priglone, the Vatican's apostolic nuncio to Mexico to offer their confession.

When the revelation brought into question links between the Church and the cartels, the nuncio was forced into giving a statement.'I received them in private and listened to them... I am obliged to keep secret that which people confide to me in private.'

Although El Chapo Guzmán seemed to be the intended victim of the attack, the practical consequences for his way of life were to be dramatic. In the public clamour for justice, the government responded with a high-profile manhunt and a $5 million (£4m) bounty on the head of every person involved in the shoot-out. More worryingly for El Chapo, though, portraits and photographs began to appear on TV screens and in newspapers. Previously unknown to ordinary Mexicans, El Chapo Guzmán was now a public figure with a price on his head. He would have to go into hiding.

In the days that followed, Guzmán kept on the move. He first headed for a ranch he had started up in Tonalá in the suburbs of Guadalajara in Jalisco state. Fearing that his life – or at the very least his freedom – was under threat, he moved out of the region to a safe house in Mexico City to take care of his business affairs. He met two unknown associates, with each of whom he deposited $200 million (£160m) in cash.

In the event of his death, disappearance or capture, one payment was to look after his family; the other was to ensure that Sinaloa cartel business could continue smoothly. He was then chauffeured to Chiapas in the south of Mexico, close to the border with Guatemala.

One of the Sinaloa's lieutenants in the area was also a colonel in the Guatemalan army; El Chapo paid him $1.2 million (£960,000) for a fake passport for himself and four close colleagues, including one of his mistresses, to hide out across the border. Now going under the name Jorge Ramos Perez, El Chapo was taken to a hotel in Tapachula on 4 June 1993 while he planned his next move. Five days later, a dawn raid saw the building surrounded by Guatemalan soldiers. Guzmán had been betrayed.

'CORN AND BEAN FARMER'

Two decades later, Otto Pérez Molina, the Guatemalan army general who had led the operation to arrest Guzmán, and who later became the country's president, was himself being tried for stealing $3.7 million (£3m) in a customs fraud scheme. His defence was that the sums being discussed were tiny compared to those he turned down from El Chapo at the time of the arrest.

He recalled the scene. 'The first thing [he] did was try and negotiate,' Pérez Molina told the court. 'The [bribe] offer we got after his capture was perhaps 10 or 15 times the amount that you're accusing me of here, and I didn't do it because it went against my principles.'

Two days later, El Chapo Guzmán boarded a military aircraft, which returned him to Mexico. Mexican Attorney General Jorge Carpizo treated El Chapo's arrest as a national triumph. 'The Mexican government has shown its ability to respond to the shameful events that have moved the entire nation and will continue to respond with the effectiveness needed in these cases,' he said. 'The current investigation shows that it is possible to halt impunity and lack of public safety.' On display in front of the media, Guzmán denied the charges of drug trafficking, murder and kidnapping. 'I'm just a corn and bean farmer who was sightseeing in Guatemala,' he claimed somewhat unconvincingly.

El Chapo was first taken to Federal Social Readaptation Centre No. 1, better known as Altiplano, in Mexico state. Initially, he received a 20-year sentence for possession of firearms, drug trafficking and the murder of

Cardinal Juan Jesús Posadas Ocampo. The latter charge was eventually dropped and his sentence reduced. On 22 November 1995, he was transferred to Federal Social Readaptation Centre No. 2, Puente Grande, in Jalisco. Although these were regarded as two of Mexico's highest-security prisons, El Chapo treated both almost as a private playground.

It was rumoured that most of Puente Grande was on his payroll; associates from the Sinaloa brought him suitcases filled with cash to use as bribes, the prison guards being little more than servants. Special meals were 'ordered' from the kitchen. Wine and liquor was freely available; for one Christmas Eve party, 110 gallons (500 litres) of wine were shipped in. On one occasion, he was said to have had the Puente Grande dining hall converted into a cinema with popcorn and candy for all. And if there was discipline to be administered, it came from El Chapo and his cohorts rather than the prison authorities.

Financial inducements were usually enough to get him what he wanted, but occasionally other measures were necessary. Inmates and guards alike tended to do as they were told when their families were discussed – or baseball bats were wielded.

He was also able to enjoy conjugal visits from his wives; both Alejandrina María Salazar Hernández and Griselda López Pérez were regular visitors. One of the prison guards was kept on a $3,000 (£2,400) monthly retainer, his task being to select prostitutes in Guadalajara bars and smuggle them back into Puente Grande; to prevent spirits flagging, a supply of Viagra was always on hand.

LIFE BEHIND BARS

It's possible to get some measure of the life El Chapo was able to lead in Puente Grande: in 2015 Jose Antonio Ortega, former lawyer for the Catholic Church in Guadalajara, described a visit he had made to Guzmán 15 years earlier.

His purpose was to interrogate the prisoner regarding the death of Cardinal Posadas Ocampo. 'The interrogation wasn't held in the usual room. We were taken into a private office and given VIP service,' he recalled. Forced to wait for more than 12 hours before El Chapo agreed to see him, he continued: 'El Chapo calmly explained to me: "Today I had a conjugal visit, and afterwards I needed to take a bath, with hot steam, to relax myself and wind down. After that I took a little nap to receive you properly…" In that moment, I realized that the man in charge of that place was El Chapo Guzmán. He was the boss of the prison.'

Journalist Anabel Hernández made similar observations. 'Mexico exists in a stew of corruption. That's what produced El Chapo Guzmán,' she claimed. 'He became so powerful in Puente Grande that one Christmas he invited his whole family for a vacation at the "resort" he had created in the maximum-security prison. His family spent an entire week there.'

Guzmán was even able to take mistresses from within the prison. He requested that one kitchen worker who caught his eye, Ives Eréndira Arreola, be transferred to his own block. At first she was reluctant, but worn down – not to say terrified – by El Chapo's advances she eventually gave in; they would engage in regular trysts inside visitors' cubicles until she'd had enough and resigned from her job. Even then, El Chapo would have his men visit her at home with large gifts of cash.

Controversially, there were also three female prisoners being held at Puente Grande at that time, among them a beautiful young ex-police officer whose head, like many before and since, had been turned by the wealth of the narcos she investigated. Zulema Yulia Hernández was serving a jail term for trafficking and armed robbery when she and El Chapo began their affair.

It would follow a similar pattern to other similar relationships he'd enjoyed in the past: obsessive desire would see the subject overwhelmed, lavished with attention and gifts of flowers, chocolates and money.

Although El Chapo was barely able to write, he would shower her with mawkish love notes penned for him by fellow inmates. They might easily have been lifted from the overwrought Mexican TV soaps that he so loved. 'Hello, *mi vida*! Zulema, darling,' went one letter that Hernández would later pass on to Mexican journalist Julio Scherer. 'I have been thinking of you at every moment and I'd like to imagine that you are happy and cheerful… When you love someone the way I love you, their good news brings you happiness too… Darling, these days my only comfort is thinking, especially thinking of you and of a day that I can hopefully live my life by your side.'

Hernándes would later recall their first sexual encounter. 'After the first time, he sent to my cell a bouquet of flowers and a bottle of whisky,' she told Scherer. 'I was his queen.'

As was often the way with El Chapo, he would begin to lose interest soon after the object of his affection had been won over. Hernández recounted her treatment at the hands of Guzmán.

When he was finished with her, he simply 'passed her around to his friends in the prison'. While she was in prison, Zulema was said to have been forced into having two abortions, during one of which she came close to bleeding to death. Stories abounded of other women being abused and raped during El Chapo's 'reign', but no investigations ever took place – hardly surprising when so many officials were being bankrolled by Guzmán.

Although she would remain one of El Chapo's mistresses, there was to be no happy ending for Zulema Yulia Hernández. After leaving Puente Grande in 2003, she would work for the Sinaloa as part of the cartel's expansion into Mexico City until her disappearance in December 2008; her body was later found in the trunk of a car with the letter 'Z' carved into her back, breasts and buttocks – the calling card of Los Zetas, then engaged in a brutal conflict with the Sinaloa.

TAKING CONTROL

In June 1995, El Chapo's co-leader in the Sinaloa cartel, Héctor Luis Palma Salazar, was involved in an air crash. On his way from Sonora to a wedding party in Guadalajara, Palma's 12-seater Lear jet crash-landed and, although he survived, he was taken into custody by the federal police attending the scene. From there, he was extradited to the United States, where he faced charges for drug trafficking and murder. El Chapo Guzmán was now firmly in control of the Sinaloa.

Even though he was locked up, the prison regime he had crafted for himself enabled business to be continued from his cell. On the ground, his brother Arturo Guzmán Loera, known as 'El Pollo' (The Chicken), carried out instructions conveyed to him either by cellphone or by one of his brother's many lawyers.

In spite of periodic conflicts with rival groups, El Chapo and the Sinaloa cartel were already the wealthiest of Mexico's drug lords by the time of his incarceration and they became increasingly prominent as the 1990s went on. The fall of the Colombian cartels, the willingness of Mexico's authorities to 'look the other way' in the name of retaining order and, later, the switch to producing and trafficking methamphetamine were all significant contributing factors.

The Colombian cartels were at war with their government, who were under pressure from (and supported by) the United States and its Drug Enforcement Agency. Pablo Escobar's Medellín, which had once supplied more than 80 per cent of the world's cocaine, fell apart after the death of its leader; on 2 December 1993, the *Bloque de Búsqueda* (Search Block), a special operations unit of the Colombian National Police, rooted out, shot and killed Escobar.

The Cali cartel, run by the Rodríguez Orejuela brothers, Miguel and Gilbert, picked up the slack and became what DEA Chief Thomas Constantine described as 'the biggest, most powerful crime syndicate we've ever known'. The Cali was more robust and business-like than the Medellín, comprising a large number of semi-autonomous cells, making the organization very hard to pin down. Their money laundering processes were also more sophisticated, featuring as they did legitimate businesses, including hotels, factories and Colombia's largest pharmacy chain Drogas La Rebaja. Most of El Chapo's contacts were with the Cali.

The authorities went after the Rodríguez Orejuela brothers with the same vigour as their rival Escobar and, in the summer of 1995, both were apprehended, although in separate incidents. 'The Cali cartel died today,' Colombia's national police chief Jose Serrano told reporters following the arrest of Miguel Rodríguez Orejuela. The country's president Ernesto Samper Pizano went further, trumpeting 'the beginning of the end of the problem of drug trafficking in Colombia'. Colombia's cocaine supply fell into the hands of smaller criminal gangs who were less able to dictate terms to the Mexican cartels.

With Escobar and the Rodríguez Orejuelas out of the way, cocaine trafficking suddenly became much more profitable for El Chapo and his cohorts.

HORRIFIC POSSIBILITY

For the remainder of the 1990s, El Chapo accepted his circumstances. Even though Puente Grande was a maximum-security jail with two full-time guards supposedly allocated to each cell, Guzmán lived life like no other prisoner. Furthermore, he felt reasonably safe from the unpredictable personal attacks of the Arellano Félix clan.

His original sentence had been reduced to 13 years, and his lawyers constantly worked towards further concessions. But as things stood, he would have expected to be released somewhere around 2006 when he could expect to resume life at the helm of the Sinaloa.

As the new millennium dawned, however, he became aware, that a dramatic change might be on the horizon. During 2000, El Chapo Guzmán and the Sinaloa's attorney Humberto Loya-Castro were both indicted in San Diego. Guzmán was charged with money laundering and trafficking cocaine into California. Furthermore, recent legislation had made the tortuous extradition process between Mexico and the United States more straightforward. There seemed to be a small but horrific possibility that he could be sent to face trial in America. That couldn't be allowed to happen.

During the evening of 19 January 2001, the prison's security cameras were disabled and the electronically controlled door to Guzmán's cell was suddenly unlocked. He was bundled into a prison laundry cart hidden under a pile of clothing, as prison guard Francisco Javier 'El Chito' Camberos Rivera pushed him outside Puente Grande, where they jumped into a car and headed towards Guadalajara. Outside the city, Guzmán asked his driver to stop the car at a petrol station and to go and buy him a bottle of water. When he returned, El Chapo and the car were gone.

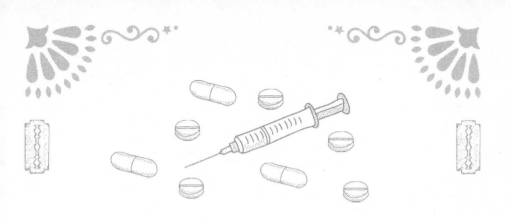

CHAPTER 4:
THE RISE OF EL CHAPO

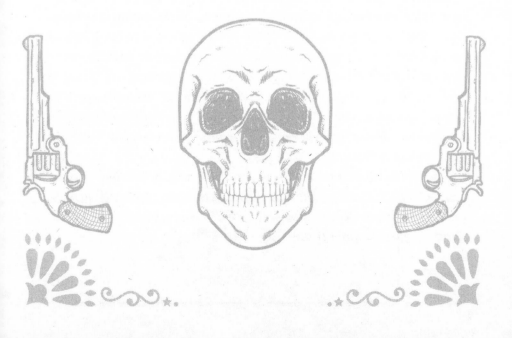

The turn of the century brought about an unexpected change in Mexico's political landscape. The presidential election overturned 71 years of rule for the Institutional Revolutionary Party (PRI) on 1 December 2000, when Vicente Fox Quesada, former governor of Guadalajara, came to power. It was a sight that no Mexican had ever seen before, an incumbent president conceding power to the opposition.

When Fox assumed office with an approval rating of 80 per cent, there was a new air of optimism within the country. Representing the centre-right National Action Party (PAN), Fox had campaigned to bring an end to the blight of corruption at the heart of Mexico's government, police and military, and to boost the economy with a programme based around investment and education. He had already shown his willingness to take a firm public line when he announced: 'The pervasive influence of dirty money has infected law-enforcement organizations and dishonest government bureaucrats.'

Yet in only his second month in office, the task before him became manifest when he suffered the embarrassment of having one of Mexico's most notorious narcos escape from what was supposed to be one of Mexico's most secure prisons.

It was the ease with which Guzmán had made his exit from Puente Grande that was so shocking. This was no audacious TV drama escape plot: El Chapo Guzmán simply bought his way out of jail.

A week after the escape, speaking at the World Economic Forum in Davos, Switzerland, President Fox responded to critics. 'The corruption of the past can't be ended overnight,' he said, 'but now we are truly trying to eradicate it.' Fox's newly appointed chief of security, Alejandro Gertz Manero, explained how the drug cartels had taunted the new administration with threats of political assassinations. He was under no illusion as to the scale of the problem. 'In our country, throughout its existence, and especially over the past few years,' he told reporters, 'forces have arisen that are much stronger and more effective than the official ones. Cloaked by political corruption for generations, they have truly become overwhelming.'

It was an astonishing admission that Mexico's crime organizations, and in particular El Chapo Guzmán's Sinaloa cartel, were more powerful than the nation's own police and military forces. Those heading the anti-drug task force in the previous administration were themselves suspected of being on cartel payrolls. Under the new regime, the Attorney General fired more than 1,400 of 3,500 federal police officers, and prosecuted a quarter of them. El Chapo's disappearance naturally sparked a nationwide manhunt, but there were also some serious questions facing those running the prison complex: the president ordered an immediate investigation into Puente Grande.

THE BIRD IS READY TO FLY

Even though he had been detained for eight years, there had been suspicions before his actual getaway that El Chapo might soon be about to attempt escape. On 18 January 2001, the Mexican Supreme Court had reached a landmark ruling on the extradition of its nationals. Although there had been an agreement between Mexico and the United States since January 1980, the Mexican government had always been reluctant to hand over convicted criminals for punishment in a foreign land. Indeed, not a single significant high-level narcotics trafficker had ever been extradited.

Early in 2001, such a shift in the landscape would have been terrifying to Guzmán; in a US maximum-security prison, he could expect a sentence that would see him incarcerated for most of the remainder of his years; he could bid farewell to the gourmet meals, cocktails, wine lists and prostitutes that his bribes currently allowed – on one occasion, he had even hired a mariachi band to be brought into Puente Grande!

More to the point, though, he would no longer be able to run the Sinaloa cartel from the comfort of a luxury prison cell. El Chapo needed to act... and act fast.

On the morning of 19 January 2001, a delegation of officials headed by Jorge Tello Peón, the country's chief of public security, visited Puente Grande having heard whispers that Guzmán was soon to make his move. Following inspection, Tello Peón demanded that his prize prisoner be moved to a higher-security wing of the prison.

Before the order could be carried out, El Chapo had gone. At 11:35pm that evening, more than an hour after Guzmán had last been checked, prison warden Leonardo Beltrán Santana was notified that the cell was empty. Had El Chapo – like the story already circulating suggested – escaped in a laundry basket? Or was the truth more prosaic? Once he'd had enough, did he merely throw cash at the right prison officials who simply allowed him to walk out through the gates?

Beltrán ordered a thorough, wing-by-wing, cell-by-cell search of Puente Grande. Yet, curiously, it was five hours before Deputy Tello Peón was informed of events.

The news headlines the following morning were an embarrassment for the new government. President Fox had been due to give a speech in El Chapo's home state of Sinaloa. 'Today I reaffirm our war without mercy against the pernicious criminal mafias,' he declared furiously. He pledged a 'great reform... so every family can sleep peacefully, so we all can live without fear of going out into the street, without assaults or humiliation, without the fear of losing everything at the hands of the criminals.'

Outraged, Tello Peón ordered an immediate investigation into security at Puente Grande. As unconfirmed rumours were doing the rounds that El Chapo had even been allowed to leave prison at weekends to visit friends and family and to conduct Sinaloa business, Tello Peón knew that there was only one way this escape could have been possible. 'All the prison bars and millions of pesos spent on security systems are useless if prisoners leave through the door,' he fumed. 'What happened is proof of the capacity of corruption, or rather structural corrosion, of national institutions by organized crime – particularly drug-traffickers.'

Seventy-three officials, guards, ancillary workers and even the warden himself, were detained for questioning. Only 'El Chito' Camberos Rivera, the guard who had driven Guzmán from Puente Grande, would actually receive a prison sentence.

The morning following the Puente Grande fiasco, the government announced a large-scale national manhunt that began with the Mexican Army searching through houses, ranches and buildings in the immediate vicinity of the prison complex. In Guadalajara, the federal police ransacked a known Sinaloa house; drugs, cash-filled briefcases and military-grade weapons were seized, but there was no sign that El Chapo had ever been there.

A tip-off from a previously used source led the police to Manzanillo, Colima on the Pacific coast; 17 houses and four ranches were searched. It was becoming clear that El Chapo Guzmán had fled the region.

Government authorities even began to fear that he might have been smuggled out of Mexico: the FBI was alerted in case he had fled across the northern border into California or Arizona; in the south, border guards were reinforced in case he had headed for Guatemala.

Guzmán, in fact, was already home among his family and Sinaloa associates in Badiraguato in the Sierra Madre. According to later court testimony from Jesús Zambada, brother of Guzmán's Sinaloa partner Ismael El Mayo Zambada, a helicopter had been organized to collect El Chapo and bring him to them at a 'semi-deserted place'. He and the brothers were then taken on a long drive to a ranch belonging to one of his top *sincerios*, Francisco Aceves Urías, known as 'El Barbarino' (The Barbarian). He reported that Guzmán was eager to get back to work. 'I'm going to start organizing my people,' he told him. 'Let's do this!'

Over the decade that followed, El Chapo Guzmán would transform himself from one of a number of Mexican *capos* (the Italian word used to describe a 'drug baron') to the most powerful narcotics-trafficker in the world. And he would do all this while evading law-enforcement agents from Mexico and the United States. 'We have personnel dedicated strictly to Chapo Guzmán. That's the importance we have placed on getting him,' an anonymous DEA official told CBS News. 'Thousands of law-enforcement personnel are exclusively focused on the entire Sinaloa operation.'

BAD BLOOD

There were considerable risks in leaving Puente Grande. Guzmán was well aware of that. Yes, the Mexican police and military and the United States DEA would be after him, but as the capo of the dominant Mexican drugs organization, El Chapo had just as many enemies among the criminal fraternity. Some within the Sinaloa had even been happier when El Chapo was managing matters from behind bars; he, in turn, was increasingly unsure of who among his cohorts and allies were still to be trusted.

There also remained bad blood and unfinished business with the Tijuana's Arrellano Félix brothers, who had made their intentions towards him clear – they wanted him dead. Both the Tijuana and Gulf organizations were making a play for the routes run by the Juárez cartel. It had been paralyzed by the loss of their leader, 'Lord of the Skies' Amada Carillo Fuentes, who had died in 1997 – while undergoing plastic surgery to alter his facial appearance – and by the arrest of General Gutiérrez Rebollo, recruited by the Mexican government to head up their anti-drug force but later discovered to be on the Carillo Fuentes payroll.

Guzmán's jailhouse mistress, Zulema Hernández, claimed that he confided his anxieties to her during their regular trysts: 'He knew that if he escaped... they might kill him.' He was now Mexico's most wanted criminal, with a $7 million (£5.6m) bounty on his head, and it was clear that his life would, for the time being at least, be constantly on the move. And that the increasingly bitter rivalries between the cartels would soon come to a head.

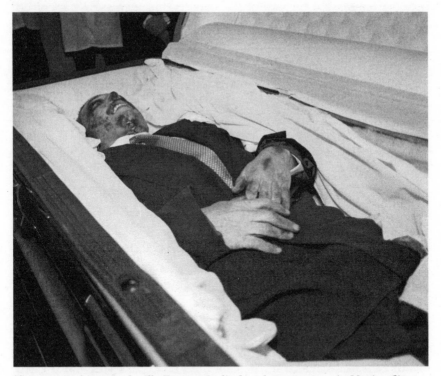

The corpse of Amada Carillo Fuentes is displayed at a morgue in Mexico City, 5 April 1997. He died of a heart attack while undergoing plastic surgery and liposuction to change his appearance.

With Guzmán back at the helm, the early years of the new millennium saw the Sinaloa cartel thriving as it continued to strengthen its hold over the Pacific trafficking routes.

The seeming inability of President Fox's National Action Party (PAN) to pursue El Chapo and his cohorts on their own soil raised questions even from within his own party. PAN's federal congressman for Sinaloa, Manuel Clouthier, angered his own government when he proclaimed: 'In Sinaloa, I have no doubt that organized crime rules. There are whole neighbourhoods controlled by criminals. Every day, there are more luxury homes built where we know they live without fear.'

During his first year on the run, Guzmán was shunted between hideouts the length and breadth of the country, but increasingly spent his time hidden in remote areas of the Sierra Madre among those he most trusted. He had access to sophisticated communications technology and was protected by army-trained gunmen and a network of informants.

In US diplomatic cables later made public by the WikiLeaks organization, Mexico's defence secretary Guillermo Galván Galván claimed that Guzmán was able to avoid detection by constantly moving 'between 10 and 15 different locations', and that he had 'a security detail of up to 300 men'. The dirt-track roads within the Golden Triangle made newcomers highly visible to the local residents, many of whom, either through bribes or intimidation – or the fact that they were making a living working for the cartel – were loyal to their leader.

To many, El Chapo was a symbolic figure, a rebel son of toil who looked after their interests and whose achievements were to be celebrated rather than condemned. According to police reports, Guzmán always travelled with his wife, Griselda López Pérez, and was under the protection of Sinaloa bodyguard Juan Mauro 'El Trece' Palomares. His movements were carefully organized in advance by former police officer Jesús Castro Pantoja. (Arrested in November 2001, Pantoja was interrogated and the video was released to the media. He admitted that he worked 'in the Chapo Guzmán organization' and that his job was 'to coordinate personal security and to serve as liaison officer'. Critically, he told them he had last seen his boss in Puebla three days earlier.)

Even though El Chapo 'owned' influential officials, he was nonetheless vulnerable and there was a series of close shaves in the year that followed his escape.

In March 2001, he hid out in Los Limones, a ranch in Santa Fe; Mexican troops launched a raid but, quite possibly after receiving a tip-off, El Chapo and his senior staff had already made their escape via helicopter two days earlier. After a brief stay in Mexico City, he was travelling in a convoy between Toluca and Santa Fe the following September when it was stopped by the Federal Preventative Police; fortunately for El Chapo, the officers searched the wrong SUV – the one carrying his brother Arturo – and he was able to slip away. One of the bodyguards arrested with his brother called him while he was in custody, warning him to leave his safe house immediately. It seemed that with his army of informants he was always able to stay one step ahead of the authorities.

UNINVITED GUESTS

The most dramatic of the attempts to recapture Guzmán took place in 2004. Informants notified federal agents that El Chapo Guzmán and El Mayo Zambada were hosting a large party on a hilltop ranch in Badiraguato, close to where El Chapo was born. Military vehicles would have struggled to deal with the dirt-track roads of Sierra Madre, so Mexican air force helicopters swooped down on the gathering and arrested a dozen or so ranch workers.

By the time they arrived, El Chapo and his men were long gone. Suspicions remained that this had not been a serious attempt to apprehend Mexico's most wanted criminal, but rather it had been intended to warn him off. On the surface, the Fox administration seemed to be taking a stronger line against the narcotics industry. There's no genuine evidence to suggest the PAN were complicit in El Chapo's activities during this time, but their interventions often seemed to benefit the Sinaloa over their rivals.

As the Arellano Félix brothers eyed up the Juárez *plazas*, Guzmán's partner El Mayo Zambada entered into an alliance with their new leader, Rodolfo Carillo Fuentes, brother of Amado. This gave the Sinaloa the opportunity to move into Tijuana, where El Mayo immediately ordered a series of high-profile executions, among them, in February 2000, Alfredo de la Torre Márquez, a police chief well known for being 'clean'. Violent crime had increased since the Arellano Félix brothers took control of the city's narcotics business, but it would escalate as the rivalry between the Sinaloa and Tijuana organizations became ever more heated.

In February 2002, Ramón Arellano Félix took his gunmen into El Mayo's home territory of Mazatlán in Sinaloa, their mission to eliminate him. They spent several fruitless days driving around the city without catching sight of Zambada. Like many in Mexico's federal police force, officers in Mazatlán were underpaid, undertrained and therefore susceptible to bribery. And many were on El Mayo's payroll.

When their car was approached by a group of police officers, guns were drawn. Ramón Arellano Félix took bullets to his chest and died 15 minutes later. Within a matter of weeks, Ramón's brother Benjamín was arrested by the Mexican army in Puebla. 'We've got this brutal organization in a choke hold,' proclaimed DEA chief of operations Michael Braun. 'We feel like we've taken the head off the snake.'

Nor were Guzmán and Zambada unhappy at this outcome. The Tijuana cartel had not, as the government claimed, been 'totally broken up', but they would never again wield the same power and influence.

Guzmán, like others, had also been eyeing up the lucrative Ciudad Juárez–El Paso trafficking route. Since the death of Amado Carillo Fuentes in 1997, this had been run by his brother Vicente, known as El Viceroy. But the Juárez cartel was no longer the powerhouse it had been a decade earlier; it had been weakened by a power struggle, and many of its members had already defected to the Sinaloa. Even though the 'federation' set up by El Mayo Zambada was still in place, the time was right to make a move on the Juárez *plaza*.

Vicente's younger brother, Rodolfo 'El Niño de Oro' (The Golden Boy), was responsible for negotiations with other cartels. He was said to have been vocal in his dislike of El Chapo and refused to accept the idea of him leading their alliance. According to the testimony of Jesús Zambada Garcia at El Chapo's trial in 2018, a meeting between the two cartels had left El Chapo outraged and insulted. 'When [Rodolfo] left, Chapo gave him his hand and said, "See you later, friend," and Rodolfo just left him standing there with his hand extended,' Zambada told the court. 'Chapo was really mad!'

He recalled that his brother, El Mayo, had gone on to say: '*Mi compa* Chapo is very upset. He said Chapo said he is going to kill him because he couldn't take Rodolfo anymore.'

Late in the afternoon of 11 September 2004, Rodolfo Carillo Fuentes, his wife and child, were leaving a multiplex cinema in Culiacán when they were attacked by gunmen. Rodolfo and his wife were killed instantly in front of their young daughter. Vicente Carillo Fuentes knew at once who was responsible – and how he would respond. The incident ended the alliance between the two cartels.

CONTRACT KILLING

El Chapo's beloved younger brother, Arturo 'El Pollo' (The Chicken), was one of his most trusted lieutenants and also a close confidant. While El Chapo was locked up, it was Arturo who had carried out his instructions from inside Puente Grande prison. On 7 September 2001, police raided a Sinaloa cartel safe house where they discovered Arturo. He was charged with conspiracy, sale of cocaine and the building of 'narcotunnels' in Tijuana.

Federal prosecutors were ecstatic. 'We are optimistic that Guzmán's capture will lead us to his brother, Joaquín.' He served his sentence at the Altiplano maximum-security prison while his brother made vain attempts to procure his release. On 31 December 2004, Arturo Guzmán was sitting in a cubicle in the call centre area where inmates were able to talk to their attorneys. At around 7pm, fellow prisoner José Ramírez Villanueva pulled out a handgun and shot him seven times. His death was immediate.

When tried for the murder in 2006, Ramírez claimed that the threats made against his family had forced him into carrying out the execution. It was never revealed who was behind it, but it was assumed to be a revenge killing ordered by Vicente Carillo Fuentes. A distraught El Chapo had his brother interred in his $1.2 million (£9.6m), five-building family mausoleum complex in Sinaloa's extraordinary 'narco-cemetery', where many of the cartel's most notorious figures have been laid to rest. This would be the impetus for a year-long turf war between the two cartels which would eventually see the Sinaloa absorbing much of the territory belonging to the Juárez cartel.

Nothing but the best: the Jardines del Humaya cemetery with its amazingly elaborate narco mausoleums where drug-traffickers are buried with luxuries such as air-conditioning and bullet-proof glass, Culiacán, Sinaloa.

In 2009, a United States National Public Radio (NPR) broadcast made claims that backed up what many had previously thought – the Mexican government had actively colluded with the Sinaloa cartel to allow them to take control of the Juárez Valley routes; one police commander interviewed even stated that his entire department had been working with the Sinaloa to overthrow the Juárez cartel.

The Mexican government denied all claims. Yet there could be no question that government targets always *seemed* to work in favour of the Sinaloa.

CHAPTER 5:
THE MEXICAN DRUG WARS

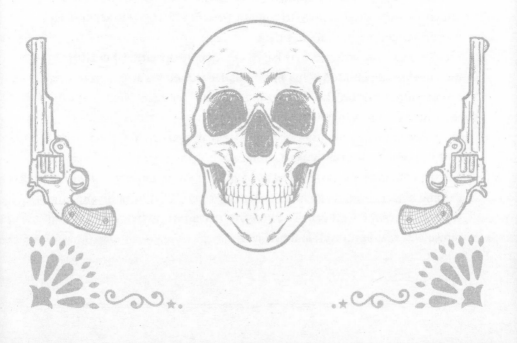

The death of El Chapo's brother Arturo would signal the start of six months of personal setbacks. In February his son Archivaldo, one of the 'Chapitos', was arrested in Jalisco and charged with money laundering. He was later released.

On 16 June 2005, El Chapo's brother Miguel Angel was arrested at a restaurant while celebrating his daughter's 15th birthday. He was charged with opening multiple bank accounts under different names in which he deposited almost 18 million pesos ($780,000/£632,000). He was sentenced to 13 years in prison.

These personal setbacks may have been deeply upsetting, but Guzmán remained single-minded in his ambitions. He turned his attention to new opportunities within the trade routes in north-eastern Mexico run by the Gulf cartel in Tamaulipas and Matamoros.

A power vacuum resulting from the 1996 arrest of Juan Garcia Ábrigo had brought Osiel Cárdenas Guillén to power. A ruthless figure, he had assassinated his close co-leader, Salvador Gómez Herrera, in 1999, earning him the nickname *Mata Amigas* (Friend Killer). But his position at the helm of the Gulf cartel was far from assured and he quickly found himself caught up in a violent turf war.

He responded by forming a brutal mercenary wing made up of army deserters from Mexico's elite *Group Aeromóvil de Fuerzas Especiales* (GAFE) special forces. Known as Los Zetas, they were trained in commando and urban warfare by Israeli and United States special forces, and acted as official bodyguards to Cárdenas. Their first commander was Arturo Guzmán Decena who had been a member of the federal judicial police; the group took its name from the 'Z1' radio code used by high-ranking police officers, as Decena had once been.

The formation of Los Zetas was a brilliant piece of strategy. They were ruthlessly professional, carrying out their operations swiftly and efficiently. They were also able to use their army backgrounds to obtain military-grade weapons and to encourage former colleagues to desert the army and join up with them. Not only did Los Zetas enable Cárdenas Guillen to cement his control of the Gulf cartel, they became an increasingly influential part of the organization.

SHOWDOWN AT THE BORDER TOWN

El Chapo was not the only one itching to take down Osiel Cárdenas Guillén and the Gulf cartel. It had been in the sights of the United States Drug Enforcement Agency since November 1999, when two federal agents (one from the DEA; one from the FBI) had been captured at gunpoint and ordered to hand over their passenger, an informant, for execution.

On Gulf territory, in the border town of Matamoros, Cárdenas and 15 of his henchmen surrounded the Americans' car and ordered them out; only when the narcos were reminded of how the US and Mexican authorities had responded to the Kiki Camarena murder were the three of them allowed to leave. 'You gringos, this is my territory,' Cárdenas shouted at them. 'You can't control it so get the hell out of here!'

With a bounty of $2 million (£1.6m) on offer, the two governments launched Operation Goldengrips to bring down Cárdenas. Their break came at the end of 2002, when a high-ranking member of Los Zetas was arrested. Former general staff intelligence officer Alejandro Lucio Morales Betancourt made a deal with the Mexican army – he would give up Cárdenas in return for immunity from prosecution. On Friday 14 March 2003, the Mexican army and special forces launched a series of raids on Matamoros.

More than 80 troops were involved in the operation, surrounding a house where Cárdenas was holding a birthday party for one of his daughters. At 9:45am, the first gunshots rang out and full-scale battle erupted.

Cárdenas attempted to escape but was caught heading for the airport. Another of El Chapo's foes had fallen. Much was made of the Cárdenas arrest. He was, after all, the first major narco to be captured on President Fox's watch. US Ambassador Tony Garza called it 'a great victory for law and order'. The DEA put out a press statement: 'It is an important arrest because it sends messages to traffickers that violence and intimidation will not protect them from law enforcement.'

After being held in high-security Altiplano prison, Cárdenas was extradited to the United States in 2007 and was given a 25-year jail sentence. Few, meanwhile, understood that with Los Zetas waiting in the wings, a full-scale war was on the verge of breaking out on Mexico's north-eastern coast.

Following the demise of a prominent rival capo, Guzmán saw the opportunity to make a move for the lucrative north-eastern trafficking routes that were run by the now severely diminished Gulf cartel. Over in Tamaulipas state, however, there was no power vacuum; Los Zetas simply swallowed up what was left of the Gulf. They were not going to cede their new strength in the region without a fight.

As he prepared his Gulf campaign, Guzmán turned to his trusted associates, the Beltrán Levya brothers. Arturo, Carlos, Alfredo, Mario Alberto and Héctor had, like El Chapo, grown up in poverty in the Sierra Madre countryside and earned their badges growing and selling their own marijuana. They now functioned as a group of 'underbosses' within the Sinaloa. Arturo Beltrán Levya in particular had proved his value through his ability to infiltrate the highest levels of Mexico's political, judicial and police institutions on behalf of the cartel.

But El Chapo knew that more military firepower was needed. He chose one of the Beltrán Levyas' top lieutenants, Edgar Valdez Villareal, known as 'El Barbie', to create a force capable of taking on Los Zetas. They would be called Los Negros (The Black Ones).

The battle for the Gulf's territories was centred around Nuevo Laredo on the north coast of Tamaulipas state. El Chapo had already made a provocative public appearance there in May 2005 at one of the city's most expensive steak and seafood restaurants.

Accompanied by heavily armed bodyguards, Guzmán walked in, then the doors were locked behind him and he announced to the 40 horrified diners that they would not be allowed to leave or use their cellphones until he had finished his meal and left the restaurant.And to make up for

After being captured in Culiacán, Sinaloa by the Mexican army in January 2008, Arturo Beltrán Levya appears before the media in Mexico City.

any inconvenience, he picked up the bill for everyone in the house that evening.

'He was there to prove a point,' FBI agent Arturo Fontes told reporters. 'He was there to let people know he's in town, that he's here to stay and he is controlling part of the [*plaza*] in Nuevo Laredo.'

Over the months that followed, the Sinaloa sent at least 200 of its troops into Nuevo Laredo and the skirmishes that had steadily been building up all year between Los Negros and Los Zetas rapidly began to intensify. By August 2005, there had been 110 drug-related executions in the city alone, 20 of them police officers.

GUNNED DOWN

The city was now a battleground. Crime reporter Guadalupe Garcia Escamilla was gunned down in the street in April shortly after signing off her morning radio show.

Most shocking of all, though, on 10 June 2005 Nuevo Laredo's new chief of police was gunned down on the day he was sworn in. The 56-year-old father of three, Alejandro Domínguez Coello, had apparently been the only applicant for the job. 'I'm not beholden to anyone. My commitment is to the citizenry,' Dominguez told reporters. 'I think those who should be afraid are those who have been compromised.'

Six hours later, gunmen wielding assault rifles opened fire on him as he climbed into his Ford pick-up truck. The Mexican government responded by sending in the army and the federal police. Gun battles even broke out at the airport as the arriving federal police were fired on by the local police, who were largely on the payroll of Los Zetas. (The entire local police force would later be stripped of their jobs and investigated for corruption.)

By 2006, the Sinaloa Cartel was recognized by the DEA as the single deadliest criminal organization faced by America. Together El Chapo Guzmán and El Mayo Zambada controlled most of the flow of cocaine, heroin and marijuana into the United States. A fourth drug market, however, had emerged at the end of the 1980s: methamphetamine, or simply 'meth'. Although part of a smaller market, meth is relatively straightforward to create: so long as you have the expertise, the precursor chemicals and the laboratory gear needed to 'cook it up', you're in business.

In Guadalajara the Colima cartel, run by José de Jesús Amezcua Contreras and his brothers Adán and Luis, had established themselves by using criminal contacts in Thailand and India to procure large stocks of ephedrine – the most difficult precursor chemical to obtain – which they then sold on at vast profit to the meth labs that operated in Mexico and the United States.

They quickly moved on to producing methamphetamine in their own labs, creating a trafficking network throughout the United States using motorcycle gangs or independent traffickers not affiliated to the cartels.

By 1995, the DEA recognized the Colima as having 'revolutionized the production of this drug by operating large-scale laboratories both in Mexico and the United States capable of producing unprecedented quantities of high-purity methamphetamine... as a result this drug is having a devastating impact in many communities across the nation.'

They suddenly became a significant target for the DEA and Mexico's own counter-narcotics agency, *Fiscalia Especial Para Atencion a los Delitos Contra la Salud* (FEADS). Lacking the political protection paid for by other drug barons, the Amezcua brothers were always vulnerable, and on 1 June 1998 Luis and Jesús were arrested in Guadalajara. Meth production continued, but without their leaders' contacts it became increasingly difficult and risky to move around.

RAPID EXPANSION

El Chapo was a natural businessman with an eye for the main chance. With the Colima gang destabilized, he took the Sinaloa into the highly profitable methamphetamine business. And this would be his own personal arm of the operation, independent of El Mayo.

Over the next five years, he cultivated his own contacts in India and China and began importing larger quantities of the precursor chemicals at vastly reduced prices. He built vast meth labs, not only hidden away in the Sierra Madre but all across Mexico.

Overseeing his meth operation was a trusted lieutenant, Ignacio Nacho Coronel, who quickly acquired the nickname 'El Ray del Cristal' (The King of Crystal). Distribution was simple; meth was trafficked alongside the Sinaloa's usual cocaine shipments. And the profit yields were tenfold: a $1 million (£800,000) consignment of ephedrine or pseudoephedrine would produce at least $10 million (£8m) worth of methamphetamine. El Chapo Guzmán was now one of the wealthiest men in Mexico.

2006 signalled the end of President Vicente Fox's administration. In anticipation of elections at the end of the year, and presumably to help the PAN remain in power, he appointed General Rolando Eugenio Hidalgo Eddy with instructions to recapture El Chapo. He knew Guzmán's greatest vulnerability was his family.

Intelligence reports suggested that Guzmán regularly visited his mother, María Consuelo Loera Pérez, at her ranch in La Tuna, Badiraguato. The general had troops from the Mexican army launch a raid, but finding no evidence of criminal activity, the soldiers ransacked the property.

The PAN won the elections, this time under President Felipe de Jesús Calderón Hinojosa. Despite hailing from the same party, the new administration adopted a very different approach to dealing with Mexico's cartels. Outraged at the escalating bloody conflicts, Calderón declared his own 'war on drugs'.

Drug-related murders had not only escalated in Tijuana, Juárez and Tamaulipas, but a particularly violent battle was breaking out in the state of Michoacán as the La Familia organization fought to break free of former allies the Los Zetas cartel. La Familia was led with an almost religious zeal by Nazario Moreno González, who published his own doctrines based on the works of Christian philosopher John Eldredge –

indeed, he made Eldredge's *Salvaje de Corazón* (Wild at Heart) required reading for all gang members, and even paid tutors to circulate and teach the text throughout the Michoacán countryside.

Although its executions were unusually brutal, the group prided itself on functioning according to a strict set of principles. Storming the Sol y Sombra nightclub in Uruapan, the heads of five Los Zetas victims were tipped on to the dance floor along with a message: 'The Family doesn't kill for money. It doesn't kill women. It doesn't kill innocent people, only those who deserve to die. Know that this is divine justice!'

TIME TO KILL

In the ever-shifting alliances between Mexico's cartels, La Familia allied with El Chapo before themselves violently splitting off into the Knights Templar cartel after the death of Moreno González. It was clear that another period of realignment among the cartels had begun; it was the beginning of the sprawling so-called Mexican drug wars, a time of bloodshed that would see hundreds of thousands perish in their wake.

Within weeks of its election, the Calderón administration responded with Operation Michoacán, the Mexican army's first large-scale deployment against the drug cartels. On 11 December 2006, 4,000 troops were sent to the state where 500 had died in drug-related violence over the previous two years.

Although El Chapo was officially both the DEA and Mexico's most wanted criminal, the government's high-risk military action in Michoacán took a good deal of the attention away from the Sinaloa. After all, the weakening of the rival cartels involved in the conflict, Los Zetas and La Familia, could only make their position stronger.

Indeed, during the Cálderon administration El Chapo Guzmán would become an internationally recognized figure: in 2009 he made his first appearance in the famous *Forbes* billionaires list, at position 701.

He would remain on the list for a further four years. *Forbes* estimated his wealth to be $1 billion (£800m), but during his 2018 trial in

New York City the prosecution claimed that he had earned almost $13 billion (£10bn). Even now, when he is locked away, conservative estimates of his current wealth are $3-5 billion (£2.4-4bn). To the outrage of both the DEA and the Mexican authorities, El Chapo Guzmán was becoming a celebrity. The president himself leapt into the fray, strongly criticizing *Forbes*. 'Magazines,' he fumed, 'are not only attacking and lying about the situation in Mexico but also praising criminals.'

This period also saw a dramatic change in El Chapo Guzmán's personal circumstances. Emma Coronel Aispuro had been born in San Francisco, California in 1989 while her mother was visiting relatives. Although a US citizen, she grew up in Mexico in the town of Canelas in Durango State. She already had strong Sinaloa cartel connections since her uncle was Ignacio 'King of Crystal' Coronel Villarreal and her father was one of Durango's many 'ranchers' who actually made their living as opium poppy farmers for the Sinaloa.

In 2007, at the age of 17, the slim and pretty Coronel met El Chapo while competing in the local Coffee and Guava beauty pageant in Canelas. He was immediately smitten.

Sharing a lesser-known side of the narco baron, she would later tell the *LA Times*: 'I would say what won me over was his way of talking, how he treated me, the way we began to get along – first as friends and from that came everything else… He tends to win over people by his manner of being, of acting, the way he treats people in general.'

Little more than a month later, at her 18th birthday party in La Angistura, Emma Coronel became 47-year-old El Chapo's third – or possibly fourth – wife. (Whether or not Guzmán ever divorced any his previous wives remains a matter for speculation.)

TAKING OUT THE OPPOSITION

As the Sinaloa continued its ascent, El Chapo Guzmán would soon have to face a new struggle from within. The Beltrán Levya brothers had been close associates of El Chapo since its formation and an indispensable part of the Sinaloa cartel's growth. But El Chapo and El Mayo were increasingly concerned at the group's growing power base.

The businesslike Guzmán was also irked in particular by the public behaviour of Arturo ('El Jefe de Jefes' – The Boss of Bosses) and Alfredo ('El Mochomo' – The Desert Ant), who threw lavish parties, and enjoyed being photographed with glamorous soap stars and singers; President Calderón soon publicly announced that he was going after the narco bosses, proving that drawing attention to themselves in such a way had been reckless.

On 21 January 2008, Mexican army troops stopped a BMW SUV driving through Culiacán. Inside was Alfredo Beltrán Leyva and three of his security guards. Also in the car were two suitcases filled with nearly $1 million (£800,000) in cash and an assortment of Rolex watches.

Arrested and quickly spirited away to Mexico City, Beltrán Levya's capture was hailed as 'a triumph in the fight against organized crime' by the Calderón administration. It would quickly be suggested that El Mochomo had been 'shopped' by El Chapo. Offering a big name to the authorities would, after all, have taken some of the heat off him.

REVENGE BY HIT SQUAD

The outraged Arturo Beltrán Levya knew he had been betrayed by Guzmán, declared war on the Sinaloa and went into a new alliance with Los Zetas. Meanwhile, the DEA would declare the Beltrán Levyas to be a cartel in their own right and thus a sanctioned organization under the US government's Kingpin Act.

On 8 May 2008, there were two separate revenge killings in two different cities, both attributed to Beltrán Levya hit squads. In Mexico City, high-ranking police commander Édgar Eusebio Millán Gómez was gunned down outside his home; with eight bullets to the chest, he died in hospital two hours later. Meanwhile, that same evening El Chapo's 22-year-old son Edgar Guzmán Lopez, a business student at the Sinaloa Autonymous University, was out with two friends and a bodyguard.

Walking through a parking lot outside the City Club supermarket on Boulevard Universitarios at the northern end of Culiacán, they were about to get into their cars when three SUVs pulled up alongside them. Fifteen masked men jumped out and began firing handguns and assault rifles. More than 50 rounds were fired and 20 parked vehicles were damaged beyond repair. Edgar Guzmán was killed instantly.

For his distraught father, it would prove to mark the flashpoint for a brutally violent conflict between the Sinaloa and the Beltrán Levyas which was to last for the next two years – until the last of the brothers had been captured or killed. The Beltrán Levya cartel would then fragment into at least ten smaller units, many of which were short-lived or were eventually swallowed up by larger organizations.

President Calderón left office at the end of 2012. In spite of governing throughout the worst global recession in living memory, his fiscal policy was generally thought to have brought economic stability.

But his legacy, as for all Mexican political leaders in modern times, would be founded on the fight against the drug cartels. His aggressive strategy might have yielded some successes, with a number of high-profile narco bosses removed from the landscape. But the destabilizing of the cartels came at a price: the escalation of violence to an unprecedented level and rising public awareness of just how powerful these organizations had become.

Like his predecessor, Calderón and the PAN party faced widespread accusations: if not actually in cahoots with the Sinaloa, it was notable how often they did seem to target the cartel's rivals. But the sheer numbers were damning. The official national statistics for homicides over the course of his six-year term were 101,199, with 60 per cent of those linked to drug crime – a rise of almost 40 per cent over the previous administration. But many believed the true figure was a great deal higher.

And like the government of former president Vicente Fox, the Calderón administration had failed to bring El Chapo to justice. How could this be? 'He is a very intelligent guy,' was the verdict of Mexican investigative journalist Javier Valdez. 'El Chapo has been able to maintain serious battles going on all over the country and still keep the business running... He is the stuff of legend too because they look and look, but they can't seem to find him.'

The 2012 general election returned power to the PRI. Enrique Peña Nieto, former governor of the state of Mexico, became the country's 57th president. Part of his campaign was about reducing the murder rate by 50 per cent over the course of his term. It was clear his intention 'for the safety of Mexico's civilian population' was to pull back from the aggressive head-on military campaigns used by the Calderón administration. Nor did he back the presence of armed United States agents on Mexican soil.

But El Chapo remained the government's number one target, and during 2013 there was a clear sense that after 13 years on the run the authorities were finally beginning to close in.

One by one, key lieutenants began to fall. In November 2013, the DEA arrested El Mayo's son, Serafín Zambada Ortiz, at the border crossing in Nogales, Arizona. A month later in Sonora state, police gunned down one of El Mayo's top hitmen, Gonzalo Inzunza Inzunza ('El Macho Prieto').

According to Mexican authorities, he was responsible for more than 80 murders. And within a month, José Rodrigo Aréchiga Gamboa ('El Chino Ántrax'), one of El Chapo's top logistics men, and also head of his crack assassins squad Los Ántrax, was captured by Dutch police as his flight from Mexico City arrived at Amsterdam Schiphol Airport.

The arrests not only enabled the US and Mexican authorities to build up a more detailed picture of the way the upper strata of the Sinaloa operated, but gave important clues as to the way El Chapo's behaviour was changing. His new young wife, Emma Coronel, was unused to rural life in the mountains and was said to be restless. Moreover, the couple had recently become parents to twin daughters, Emali and Maria Joaquina. Wiretaps and tips from informants suggested that Guzmán was beginning to venture more frequently out of isolation in the Sierra Madre and head for Culiacán and the beach town of Mazatlán.

BETRAYED

With the Mexican authorities certain that they were now hot on the trail, marines began a methodical sweep through Culiacán at the start of 2014, caving in the doors of suspected Sinaloa safe houses and seizing stores of drugs, cash and weapons. They received a tip-off from one of El Chapo's bodyguards, who was under arrest, that on 16 February Guzmán would be visiting the house of one of his ex-wives in Culiacán.

He was indeed at the home of Griselda Guadalupe López when Mexican troops attempted to smash their way in. The steel-reinforced front door proved too difficult and by the time they'd entered, Guzmán had disappeared into a network of tunnels that passed through six adjoining houses and thus he made his way south to Mazatlán, the beach resort where he planned to see his twin daughters.

The break the authorities needed came less than a week later when the DEA traced a mobile phone signal from one of El Chapo's bodyguards to a location in Mazatlán. At 3:45am on 22 February, 10 military trucks carrying more than 60 Mexican naval marines made their way to the Hotel Miramar, a 20-storey seafront condominium on Avenida del Mar.

Intelligence suggested that El Chapo was in Room 401 on the fourth floor. Subduing Guzmán's bodyguard at the entrance to the floor, the marines stormed the apartment to find El Chapo lying on the bed next to Emma Coronel. He was struck four times as he resisted arrest – photographs would later emerge of Guzmán, handcuffed and kneeling with cuts on his face and shoulders. He was immediately flown to Mexico City and on arrival was paraded before the waiting media. Gripped on either side by Mexican marines, he was marched to a helicopter that would take him to Altiplano prison.

Guzmán's recapture made headline news across the globe. United States Attorney General Eric Holder called the arrest 'a landmark achievement, and a victory for the citizens of both Mexico and the United States'. Mexico's ambassador to the United States, Eduardo Medina Mora, said that the two governments had been working together on the case for months, but no decision had been taken as to whether Guzmán would be extradited to the United States.

But with the celebrations came words of warning. 'The takedown of Chapo Guzmán is a thorn in the side of the Sinaloa cartel, but not a dagger in its heart,' commented Professor George Grayson, a specialist in the war on drugs at the College of William and Mary in Williamsburg, Virginia.

Even without El Chapo, the Sinaloa still had formidable leaders; after all, the authorities had never come close to taking El Mayo Zambada. And nor have they yet.

DISAPPEARING ACT

El Chapo's prison experience would be in stark contrast to his time in Puente Grande. He now lived in solitary confinement 23 hours of the day with just one hour of outdoor exercise and he was allowed to communicate during his judicial hearings only. Even his prison guards were forbidden to speak with him.

On 17 April 2014, the country's attorney general, Jesús Murillo Karam, confirmed that Mexico had no intention of extraditing Guzmán to the United States. The 58-year-old narco would more than likely be spending the remainder of his life at Federal Social Readaptation Centre No. 1 – Altiplano.

The Mexican government savoured its triumph. 'We think he's being perfectly guarded and watched and we don't think it's necessary to do anything else,' said the interior minister, Miguel Angel Osorio Chong. 'He will be very isolated. He won't be allowed to continue with his operations.'

On 11 July 2015 at 20:52, prison security cameras showed El Chapo receiving his medication, and walking over to his bed, where he appeared to remove his shoes. He then walked across to the shower and toilet area, behind a low dividing wall… and vanished. Once again, Joaquín El Chapo Guzmán Loera was the world's most wanted criminal.

Now you see him now you don't: view of the shower from which El Chapo escaped into a 1 mile/1.6 km-long underground tunnel in July 2005.

CHAPTER 6:
THE ACTRESS AND THE NARCO

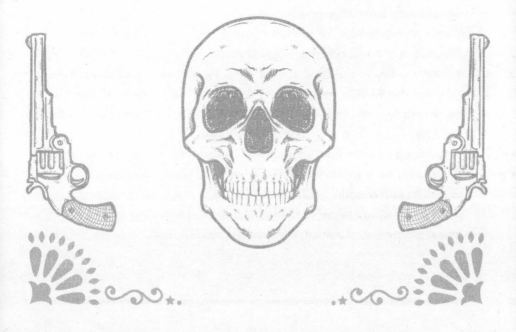

The news that El Chapo Guzmán had escaped from prison for a second time was a huge embarrassment to the government of President Enrique Peña Nieto. Federal Social Readaptation Centre No. 1 'Altiplano' was Mexico's most prominent high-security prison; its three-foot-thick walls were capable of withstanding an RPG (rocket-propelled grenade) attack and blocking a cellphone signal. It was thought to be impenetrable.

And yet on Sunday 12 July 2015 – the day after Guzmán slipped to freedom for a second time – photographs of a highly sophisticated 1 mile/1.6 km-long escape tunnel were emblazoned across the front pages of the world's press and on the screens of TV news broadcasts; more than one news source described it as an *Escape from Alcatraz* for the 21st century. It was a national humiliation.

The news reached President Enrique Peña Nieto during a transatlantic flight to France, where a four-day state visit had been planned. Only a year earlier, he had remarked that should El Chapo stage a second successful jailbreak, 'it would be more than unfortunate, it would be unforgivable.' Those words would come back to haunt him.

On arrival in Paris, he was inundated with questions from an incredulous press. In an understated response, he described the escape as 'a very unfortunate event... an affront to the Mexican state'. He was, he continued, 'indignant and deeply concerned about the escape of one of the most wanted criminals in Mexico and the world'.

Social media, meanwhile, was remorseless in its mockery of the Mexican government. One popular meme showed a photograph of Guzmán with the caption: 'That awkward moment when El Chapo went out on Saturday and you didn't!' Plenty of others sourced *The Simpsons*' hapless Chief Wiggum and his officers: *No se preocupen, nuestras profesionales y competentes autoridades están ya buscando a El Chapo* ('Don't worry, our professional and capable authorities are searching for El Chapo').

As journalist Héctor Aguilar Camín remarked in the newspaper *El Universal*: 'They say that in politics you can make a comeback from anything except looking ridiculous. El Chapo Guzmán has made the Mexican government look ridiculous!'

The implications went beyond the state of Mexico's prison security, calling into question the future of President Peña Nieto's administration and its potential to affect the country's relationship with the United States.

Guzmán's arrest in February 2014 had been lauded by US Attorney General Eric Holder as 'a landmark achievement' in the government's 'kingpin' strategy to target the leading players in Mexico's drugs cartels. It seemed proof that the Mexican government was not only willing but also able to bring down the most powerful of drugs barons: Peña Nieto's administration had presided over the capture of leading figures within the Los Zetas, Beltrán Levya, Juárez and Knights Templar cartels, all of whom had managed to evade his predecessor, Felipe Calderón.

Yet Peña Nieto's security policy had already come under fire following the abduction of 43 student protesters in Mexico City the previous year; evidence had emerged that the local mayor and corrupt police officers had handed the students over to *Guerreros Unidos*, a splinter group of the Beltrán Levya cartel; they were promptly executed.

GOVERNMENT SHORTCOMINGS

The incident shocked the Mexican public, especially following the discovery of a letter apparently signed by many of the students before their disappearance, describing fears that the mayor would have them killed. The federal government was forced to intervene. The mayor, José Luis Abarca, his wife and 40 police officers and assorted gang members were arrested and imprisoned. Yet by its tardy response and poorly conducted investigation the government managed to lose a great deal of public goodwill.

There was also suspicion within the United States Drugs Enforcement Agency that the Sinaloa cartel was out of control and was using its immeasurable wealth to buy the protection of government, police and military officials. Short of taking unilateral action within Mexico itself, the United States was dependent on the Mexican government to apprehend high-ranking criminals like El Chapo and others responsible for most of the illegal narcotics crossing the border – even if its requests for extradition were frequently denied.

Publicly, the new US Attorney General, Loretta Lynch, made supportive noises, assuring the world that the White House 'shared the government of Mexico's concern', and that they were ready to 'provide any assistance that may help support his swift recapture'.

But behind the scenes there was frustration, not least because the Peña Nieto administration had chosen to make a national 'statement' by capturing and incarcerating the world's most notorious criminal rather than permitting him to be extradited to face charges in the United States. Were Guzmán to be recaptured, the Mexican government would surely come under extreme pressure to hand him over.

President Peña Nieto immediately instructed his interior minister Miguel Osorio Chong to return from Paris to Mexico City, where he would take charge of one of the biggest criminal manhunts in the country's history. A 60-million peso ($2.6 million/£2.1m) bounty was offered for information leading to El Chapo's capture. 'We are talking about an enemy of society who has done great damage to Mexico,' Chong told reporters. 'There will be no let-up in the efforts to recapture him.' Yet the authorities were also well aware that if he found his way back to the mountains of Sinaloa, his near-mythical status might make him almost impossible to locate.

BLIND SPOT

The unfolding story of El Chapo's escape reflected increasingly poorly on Altiplano's officials. At a press conference given by national security commissioner Monte Alejandro Rubido, reporters were told that after 8:52pm on Saturday, 11 July, they became 'suspicious' when Guzmán could no longer be seen on prison cameras; the surveillance system was designed to leave only those blind spots required to fulfil human rights, one of which was in the shower cubicle.

A CCTV video was released to the media showing Guzmán's final moments in the prison; with no hint of drama, he can be seen changing his shoes and walking to the shower behind a low dividing wall... at which point he vanishes.

As guards began to investigate they found a hidden square hole in the shower room floor with a ladder that dropped 10 feet (3 m) into a narrow tunnel. At 5 ft 6 in (1.7 m), the tunnel was the same height as the stocky Guzmán and equipped with PVC tubing to supply ventilation. This was a high-tech operation.

A motorcycle had been adapted to run on rails along the 1 mile/ 1.6 km-long tunnel; it had evidently been used to transport mining tools during its construction and to excavate the earth. Rubido suggested that the motorcycle was also used to enable Guzmán to make his final speedy escape.

Interior minister Osorio Chong also offered one further extraordinary detail: 'It was designed with sophisticated technology that allowed him to get out in a lot less time than it took the security forces to follow him,' he told reporters. 'The tunnel had electricity, and as he passed through it he broke the light bulbs, making the search operation more complicated.'

There were too many questions that begged an answer. In its front-page story two days after the escape, Mexico City newspaper *Reforma* pointed out that the machinery required to excavate such a tunnel would have made the ground shake violently and yet, it seems, nobody felt a single tremor; nor did anyone notice the 3,250 tons (2,950 tonnes) of dirt that had been removed. And how, without access to detailed architectural plans, were its builders able to locate the *exact* off-camera position in the shower block where the tunnel would have to end? The inference was hardly surprising: none of this could have been achieved without collusion.

Osorio Chong announced that an official investigation would take place. 'Every federal, state or municipal official that participated in these events will be punished. Everybody involved in the escape will fall.'

Political analyst and former head of the Mexican intelligence agency Guillermo Valdés was brutal in his assessment of events to the *Guardian* newspaper. 'It demonstrated the weakness of institutions in which a high-security jail can be penetrated through a mixture of corruption, ineptness and the operational effectiveness of organized crime. The state looks putrefied.'

As soon as Guzmán's escape was discovered, the prison facility was placed in lockdown, road checkpoints were erected and helicopters scoured every inch of the surrounding area. International warnings were raised to prevent him fleeing the country by air or sea, or crossing the border in the south to Guatemala. Flights from Toluca airport were cancelled while the military occupied much of Mexico City airport.

In the immediate aftermath of Guzmán's escape, 31 of the prison's 120 employees were detained for questioning. Two of the directors of the Altiplano prison were removed from their positions and later arrested. At least 20 other officials were taken into custody, including

Celina Oseguera Parra, the former head of Mexico's federal prison service, two members of Mexico's secret service and two prison control room employees, who were accused of not raising the alarm once it was discovered that Guzmán had escaped.

For all the numerous reported sightings, Guzmán seemed to have pulled off the most impressive of vanishing acts. In spite of the numbers involved in the manhunt, Guillermo Valdés was certain, just a matter of days after the jailbreak, that unless the government were to 'get very lucky' or El Chapo made a 'stupid mistake' it was unlikely he would be recaptured easily. As it happened, however, hubris would play a big hand in sowing the seeds of El Chapo Guzmán's eventual downfall.

TALKING UP A STORM

Two years before El Chapo's second arrest, Mexican television soap star Kate del Castillo had put up a lengthy social media posting that included controversial remarks about Guzmán. The 40-year-old actress had made her name starring in the popular telenovela *La Reine del Sur* (The Queen of the South) and had recently been listed as one of the 25 most influential Hispanic women by *People en Español* magazine. She was also the ambassador for the Mexican Commission on Human Rights and frequently spoke publicly on the subject of human trafficking. And one of her most prominent fans was none other than El Chapo Guzmán – indeed, DVD boxed sets of *La Reine del Sur* were found when his safe house was stormed by the police the first time he was arrested.

Nearing midnight on 9 January 2012, del Castillo poured herself a glass of wine, sat down at her laptop, and began a lengthy post to her massive social media following.

Typing into a program called Twextra, which enabled long postings to be distributed to her Twitter followers, she began to free-associate on a wide range of 'heavy' subjects – love, sin, heaven, the Pope – before turning her attention to El Chapo, at that time still at large following his 1991 jailbreak. 'Today I believe more in El Chapo Guzmán than I do

Mexican soap queen Kate del Castillo poses with a bottle of her own tequila brand Honor *in a press conference called by the attorney general after her infamous meeting with El Chapo Guzmán.*

in the governments that hide truths from me, even if they are painful, who hide the cures for cancer, AIDs, etc., for their own benefit.' Getting into her stride, del Castillo flicked on her Caps Lock key: 'MR. CHAPO, WOULDN'T IT BE COOL IF YOU STARTED TRAFFICKING WITH THE GOOD?… COME ON SEÑOR, YOU WOULD BE THE HERO OF HEROES. LET'S TRAFFIC WITH LOVE, YOU KNOW HOW.' She signed off, 'I love you all, Kate,' hit the Send button and turned in for the night. She had no idea of the storm she had unleashed.

In the weeks that followed, her tweets were the subject of talk shows and newspaper editorials as the Mexican public endlessly debated whether she was publicly defending the brutal drug lord who still topped the world's 'most wanted' criminal listings.

Typical of the reactions were those of Mexican publishing mogul Carlos Marín who branded her remarks as 'truly stupid… this beautiful, lovely, great actress,' he concluded, was 'encouraging the commission of crime.'

The furore gradually calmed, leaving del Castillo with nothing more than a slightly tarnished reputation. What she could not have realized was that her late-night social media rant had come to the attention of El Chapo himself.

SPECIAL PROJECT

The daughter of screen legend Eric del Castillo and film producer Kate Trillo del Castillo, she came from a prominent Mexican film dynasty. In July 2014, her mother received a call from a man claiming to be a film producer who said he had a project he knew would interest her daughter.

Within days, Kate del Castillo, who now lived in Los Angeles and was currently filming a Mexican narco-drama in Miami, began receiving emails from the mystery figure. Initially she was dismissive; it was only when he identified himself as Andrés Granados Flores – *Soy licenciado de Señor Joaquín Guzmán Loera*. ('I am Señor Joaquín Guzmán Loera's lawyer.') – that she began to take the contact seriously.

By this time, Guzmán had been recaptured and was locked away in his Altiplano prison cell, yet he nevertheless seemed able to continue controlling his assorted businesses interests with ease. Granados Flores sealed the deal when he told del Castillo that his client was a fan and that he wished to discuss with her the prospect of making a film about El Chapo's life.

On 29 September 2014, Kate del Castillo boarded a private plane in Miami which took her to an airstrip on the outskirts of Mexico City. There she was met by Granados Flores and a second lawyer, Óscar Manuel Gómez Núñez. Although El Chapo had instructed them to take her to one of the city's most expensive restaurants, the actress was concerned that she might encounter the paparazzi, and so they settled on a modest, secluded roadside diner.

Guzmán, it transpired, had wanted to make contact with her a few days after her original tweet but was unable to find an address. 'He wanted to send you flowers,' the lawyers told the astonished actress.

The pitch was one she found hard to believe: although El Chapo had, they claimed, received numerous offers from Hollywood, he wanted to give *her* the exclusive rights to his life story. When she asked why she had been chosen, the response was simple: 'Because you're very brave. Because you're outspoken. Because you always tell the truth, even when it's about the government. Because you come from a great family. And because [El Chapo] is a fan of yours.'

Del Castillo saw such exclusivity as a massive opportunity, even if at that point she was unsure whether to make a documentary or a drama. Guzmán's preference, on the other hand, was quite clear. 'He wanted a big movie, and he wanted me to star in it.'

She discussed the project with two Argentinian producers, Fernando Sulichin and José Ibáñez, and conveyed their interest to Guzmán's lawyers. In December 2014, del Castillo received a gushing handwritten letter from Guzmán himself in which he thanked her for speaking out on his behalf. 'I love your acting, you really go for it. I congratulate you. I imagine acting can't be so easy, *amiga*. I hope to say hello to you in person someday. Hopefully soon.'

On the business in hand he was also clear: 'With respect to the rights, I want it to be clear that you are the one that decides everything that is done, what you want and what you don't want.'

A few weeks later, on 9 January 2015, witnessed by a notary at Altiplano prison, El Chapo Guzmán signed a contract assigning her the rights to produce a film about his life story.

THINGS BEGIN TO MOVE

Six months later, when El Chapo Guzmán pulled off his most extraordinary escape, del Castillo realized that her exclusive would now have escalated in value. Fernando Sulichin had been discussing El Chapo's jailbreak with Hollywood actor and director Sean Penn. He mentioned in passing that he knew a Mexican actress who was in close contact with Guzmán and Penn asked if it would be possible to arrange a meeting.

Penn was also a political activist with a well-documented interest in left-wing political causes within South and Central America. To the annoyance of conservative figures within the United States, he had formed friendships with Hugo Chávez, the socialist leader of Venezuela, and Cuban president Raúl Castro. It was clear to del Castillo and her two producers that the project would have a far greater chance of being made if a Hollywood 'name' like Penn was attached.

A lunch meeting in Santa Monica suggested that Penn initially had little interest in being involved in del Castillo's film, but he was excited at the prospect of being able to meet the subject in person.

Through Guzmán's lawyers, del Castillo had meanwhile been able to begin communicating with El Chapo via a pair of BlackBerry cellphones using the BBM messaging service. To the embarrassment of all parties, these messages would later be leaked in full to the press; their contents might not have been earth-shattering but they clearly indicated that Guzmán was becoming more than a little infatuated with the beautiful telenovela star.

He insisted on buying her a phone by which they could communicate – which entailed a comically unlikely discussion between El Chapo and his lawyers about the merits of Apple iPhones, Samsung Galaxies and BlackBerries – and remarked without irony that a pink model would be appropriate for a lady. He also insisted that she came to visit him in Sinaloa. ('I really want to meet you and become really good friends. You're the best thing in the world. We'll be great friends. Find out when you can return to Mexico... I will take care of everything so that you don't need anything... Trust that you'll be taken care of. I will take care of you more than my own eyes.')

Later messages even begin to take on an obsessive tone: 'Hopefully you can come soon so that I can attend to you, so that you can tell me what you want to eat and I can have it ready for you, to take care of my friend, the best in this world and the most gorgeous... I love and admire you. Bye.'

During one of the conversations she told the lawyer that she would like to bring Sean Penn along with her, who she still hoped might become involved in the project; in turn, she explained to El Chapo that Penn was the 'most recognized actor in the United States'. Guzmán had clearly never heard of Penn, nor did he seem to have a great deal of interest in meeting him, but agreed: 'Yes, let her bring the actor, and if she thinks she needs to bring more people, let her bring them, whatever she wants.'

Penn had meanwhile contacted publisher Jann Wenner, who jumped at the opportunity of an exclusive interview with the world's most wanted criminal for his *Rolling Stone* magazine. (Del Castilla would later claim that she'd had no idea of Penn's planned article; she publicly called his claim that it had been discussed at their first meeting 'total and complete bullshit'.)

JOURNEY INTO THE UNKNOWN

On 2 October 2015, Penn, del Castillo and her two producers took a privately chartered eight-seater jet (booked by the actress at a cost of $33,720/£27,000) to Guadalajara, where they were met in their hotel by El Chapo's son, Alfredo Guzmán. They were ordered to leave their phones and laptops in their rooms and were whisked away to a dirt airfield an hour-and-a-half outside the city, where they boarded two waiting, single-engine planes.

Penn later recalled the journey. 'We had not been blindfolded, and any experienced traveller might have been able to collect a series of triangulated landmarks to re-navigate the journey.' It was a turbulent flight that ended two hours later on an impromptu landing strip. There was a further gruelling, seven-hour drive by SUV through Sinaloa's mountain forests.

When the convoy was stopped at a military checkpoint, Penn noted the reaction when Alfredo Guzmán lowered his passenger window. 'The soldiers back away, looking embarrassed, and wave us through. Wow... The power of a Guzmán face. And the corruption of an institution.' (Del Castillo would later maintain that this scene, like others described in the final published article, did not take place.)

They reached their final destination, a row of nondescript run-down bungalows outside the small town of Cosalá, where they were greeted by a smiling El Chapo Guzmán. Their host was smartly dressed with a shiny silver-and-blue patterned silk shirt neatly tucked into pressed black jeans. 'He appears remarkably well-groomed and healthy for a man on the run,' Penn recalled.

As expected, Guzmán was visibly thrilled to meet Kate del Castillo, greeting her, in Sean Penn's words, 'like a daughter returning from college'. He would be attentive to her throughout the seven hours of their meeting.

GUARDED CONVERSATION

A buffet of tacos, enchiladas, chicken, rice, beans and fresh salsa had been prepared and they were seated at a picnic table along with Guzmán's wife, Emma Coronel, and his lawyers; a small coterie of security guards remained visible.

The party, in turn, was encircled by a private regiment of more than 100 soldiers; the world's most wanted man was leaving nothing to chance. Guzmán poured tequila from a bottle of del Castillo's newly launched own brand, which she had brought him as a gift, and made a toast. 'I don't usually drink,' he declared, 'but I want to drink with you!' Penn was formally introduced to Guzmán, who seemed bemused that he was unable to speak Spanish. Throughout the interview that followed, del Castillo would act as his translator.

Unlike many of the cartel barons of his generation, who viewed solitude and privacy as the most effective defence against the authorities (corrupted officials notwithstanding), Guzmán was fascinated – obsessed even – with his growing profile among the American public. He seemed delighted when told that Penn had just watched the special edition of the documentary *Chasing El Chapo* on television the night before arriving in Mexico, and shared a chuckle in his native tongue for the benefit of his colleagues.

Much of the intended serious intent behind Penn's interview fell by the wayside as Guzmán was happy to boast openly of his exploits and financial muscle. He was fascinated at the way the film industry worked but – unsurprisingly for a man accustomed only to the highest of profit margins – unimpressed with its potential to further fill his coffers. He claimed to have invested in the global energy sector through a number of unnamed corrupt major corporations but added that opportunities were limited given the nature of his funds.

He was entirely unapologetic about the source of his wealth. 'I supply more heroin, methamphetamine, cocaine and marijuana than anybody else in the world. I have a fleet of submarines, airplanes, trucks and boats.' Guzmán was also clear that he was meeting a demand: 'If there was no consumption, there would be no sales.'

At times, Penn struggled to square the contradictions of the man sitting across the table. 'This simple man from a simple place, surrounded by the simple affections of his sons to their father, and his toward them, does not initially strike me as the big bad wolf of lore.' Yet Guzmán, the world's most wanted criminal, exuded the confidence of a man used to having his instructions followed swiftly and to the letter.

Penn recalled the sense of wellbeing they all felt during the time they spent together. 'There is the pervasive feeling that if there were a threat, [he] would know it.'

At the same time, though, it was impossible to ignore the fact that this was the same man who had calmly and without compunction ordered the executions of rivals and associates he no longer trusted.

Penn asked to stay for a further two days to conduct additional interviews, assuring his host that – as was agreed with *Rolling Stone* – he would have final approval of the article before publication. Guzmán told him this would not be possible but offered to meet again in eight days.

Well into the early hours, El Chapo turned to the exhausted del Castillo: '*Amiga*, I think you have to go to sleep.' He took her arm and escorted her to her sleeping quarters in one of the other bungalows. Although she briefly feared for her safety, he remained courteous and thanked her, in her words, 'for giving me one of the best days of my life'.

PHOTO OPPORTUNITY

When Guzmán returned to the party, Penn was aware of a change in mood among El Chapo's security force who now showed visible armed presence. Penn requested a photograph to authenticate the meeting for *Rolling Stone*'s editor: 'It would be best if we are shaking hands, looking into the camera, but not smiling,' he requested. Guzmán agreed. (The impact of the photograph is an indicator of Guzmán's growing cult status in the United States: when it was eventually shared with the world, along with the publication of Penn's article, El Chapo's silk patterned shirt – $128 [£100] from Los Angeles boutique Barabas – became one of the hottest fashion items of the year!)

At around 4am, El Chapo signalled that the night was over and thanked Penn and the two producers for their visit. He confirmed that they would meet again eight days later. Guzmán and his security guards boarded their jeeps and drove away into the darkness.

Two hours later, Penn's sleep was interrupted when they were told they must leave immediately because a heavy rainstorm was forecast. They set out on the arduous journey back to their hotel in Guadalajara, and the following day for their return flight to Los Angeles. Penn would not see El Chapo again.

The heightened security that Penn had sensed within El Chapo's command centre was not something he had just imagined. The media

Picture on the website of Rolling Stone *magazine featuring El Chapo and Sean Penn.*

would later report that a day after the meeting a cellphone signal was tracked to a ranch outside Cosalá, leading to an armed attack by Mexican marines in military helicopters on 6 October.

Thirteen communities within Sinaloa were raided simultaneously creating panic and causing families caught up in the chaos to flee into the mountains. A dozen arrests were made, but all that could be found of the departed were abandoned clothing and phones belonging to Guzmán and his guards. The media reported that El Chapo had been injured in the incident, but he later reported to del Castillo via BBM that this was much exaggerated: 'Not like they said. I only hurt my leg a little bit.'

Even as the DEA and the Mexican military seemed to be closing in on Guzmán, he remained in BBM contact through his lawyers with the actress. When it became clear that no further meeting with Guzmán would be taking place, Sean Penn prepared a list of questions that Guzmán said he would answer via video.

On 5 December, a courier delivered a package to a location in New York City. It was an envelope containing a phone on which there appeared a 17-minute video of El Chapo responding evasively or half-heartedly to some of Penn's questions. As agreed, a draft copy of the article was translated and sent by del Castillo to El Chapo's lawyers. The reply was swift: '*Amiga*, I approve.'

CLOSE CALL

El Chapo Guzmán quickly tired of life in the Sinaloa mountains and instead made his way to the coastal city of Los Mochis. Construction crews working on a house in an affluent area of the city, along with reports of armed civilians, began to arouse suspicions. The authorities placed the building under surveillance. Telephone conversations about the imminent arrival of 'Grandma' were intercepted, and it soon became clear that this was a code word for an important figure – at first thought to be a high-ranking Sinaloa cartel assassin.

It was reported that the gunmen had returned to the house, which led to the launch on 8 January 2016 of Operation Black Swan. In a dawn raid, Mexican marines stormed the house. Five of Guzmán's guards were killed in the shoot-out, but El Chapo and his lieutenant, 'El Cholo Iván' Gastélum, made use of the building's carefully crafted escape route, disappearing through a hidden door in the back of a walk-in wardrobe and eventually emerging into the outside world through a manhole. From there, they made their escape in a stolen car.

With the state police on immediate alert, the vehicle was stopped 20 km (12.5 miles) south of Los Mochis while making its way to the town of Juan José Ríos, by four federal police officers. After the cops turned down bribes of cash and property, Guzmán and Gastélum were place under arrest. Fearing that Sinaloa cartel hitmen were already making their way to the area to free El Chapo, the police officers were told to take their prisoners to a motel in the town where they would be handed over to the marines.

Guzmán was subsequently taken to Los Mochis airport and transported to Mexico City, where a waiting naval helicopter returned him to Altiplano, the maximum-security prison from which he had absconded six months earlier.

President Peña Nieto offered the nation a simple message: 'Mission accomplished, we have him. I wish to inform the Mexican people that Joaquín Guzmán Loera has been captured.' United States Attorney General Loretta Lynch praised her Mexican counterparts who, she commented, 'have worked tirelessly in recent months to bring Guzmán to justice'.

Later that day, Mexico's Attorney General, Arely Gómez González, would tell reporters that El Chapo had been tracked for months, fuelling speculation that US intelligence and the Mexican Navy might have located him by tracking Sean Penn and Kate del Castillo. 'He contacted actresses and producers, which was part of one line of investigation.' When del Castillo heard the report, she was horrified: 'I wanted to die.'

Collared by the long arm of the law: El Chapo is taken back to Altiplano prison after being recaptured In January 2016.

In the wake of events, Sean Penn's *Rolling Stone* article was published two days earlier than planned on the day following the arrest. The ethics of the interview were heavily criticized, and as a work of journalism the rambling 10,000-word piece was widely derided.

A week later, Penn felt compelled to talk publicly on the subject, not least since his supposed role in locating El Chapo was being widely reported, as well as the possible legal repercussions facing both him and del Castillo. 'Let me be clear. My article has failed,' he told CBS's *60 Minutes.* 'The entire discussion about this article ignores its purpose, which was to try to contribute to this discussion about the policy in the war on drugs.'

He went on to deny the idea that he was somehow involved in Guzmán's capture, and added that Mexican government officials were 'clearly very humiliated by the notion that someone found him before they did... We're not smarter than DEA or the Mexican intelligence. We had a contact upon which we were able to facilitate an invitation.' Asked whether the Mexican government had 'wanted to encourage the cartel to put you in their crosshairs', he replied that he thought they had. But he denied that he was fearful for his life.

As a major star, Kate del Castillo was given a far harder ride in her own country, especially when her text messages with Guzmán were leaked to the media – most likely by the Mexican government itself.

It was clear that they would be targeting her for further investigation, including money laundering and the suggestion that through her film project she might have been guilty of financial collusion with El Chapo; on the advice of her lawyers, she remained in Los Angeles and didn't return to her native Mexico for the next two years. No charges were ever brought against the actress.

Following the election of President Andrés Manuel López Obrado on 1 December 2018, she finally returned to her homeland where she immediately filed a $60 million (£50m) lawsuit against the Mexican government for launching an illegal investigation. It had, she claimed, lost her both acting and business opportunities. After two years in which her life had been turned upside down, she told the Mexican media that she now had no interest at all in trying to make a film about El Chapo Guzmán.

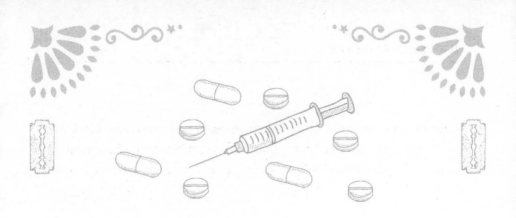

CHAPTER 7:
THE TRIAL OF
THE CENTURY

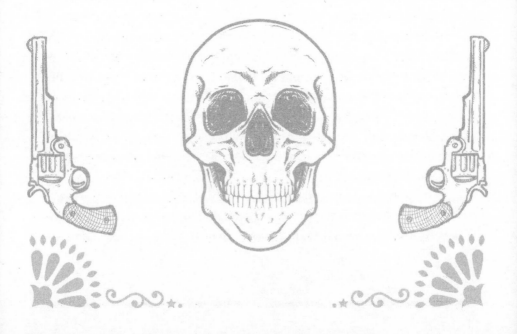

A year of renovations to a luxury house on the corner of Río Quelite Street and Jiquilpan Boulevard in the affluent Las Palmas zone of Los Mochis aroused the suspicions of neighbours and other local residents. The house had been sold in 2013 by a Mormon couple to an unknown buyer who immediately set about gutting the property. Tall, whitewashed walls with mounted CCTV cameras were erected, surrounded by densely planted olive trees making it difficult to see the house from the road.

Stranger still, it then remained empty for the following year. Eventually a flurry of arrivals – removal lorries, decorators, cleaners – at the property in the final months of 2015 suggested to local police that a VIP was on his way. El Chapo's lieutenants, including security chief Orso Iván Gastélum, had advised against any move away from the Sierra Madre mountains. Los Mochis was, after all, not even in 'friendly' territory, the north of Sinaloa having previously seen the Beltrán Levya cartel successfully gain a foothold in the area.

And barely 655 feet (200 m) along the road, a heavy police presence was already visible as the property belonging to the mother of Sinaloa's governor was provided with 24-hour security. Yet there are plenty of theories as to why El Chapo considered venturing north. His power base had begun to weaken and with it went some of the political influence that had protected him so effectively.

It was also a clear statement of intent: El Chapo Guzmán wanted his rivals to understand that he was planning to reassert his control over the area – the armoured cars, rocket-launchers and other military-grade weaponry seized after his capture suggested that he was readying himself for a fight.

As it happened, Los Mochis was spared from becoming what could have been the centre of a brutal turf war when Mexican marines launched their dawn raid on the property on 8 January 2016. Within 24 hours, El Chapo Guzmán was back at Altiplano, the maximum-security prison from which he had made his sensational escape six months earlier.

Within days of Guzmán's incarceration, Mexican agents assigned to Interpol had served two arrest warrants notifying him that he was to stand trial in the United States and that the extradition procedure was to be launched immediately. This, it quickly became clear, was hardly a straightforward process. 'It may take one year or longer,' reported Manuel Merino, the head of Mexico's extradition office.

During a radio interview given during the media frenzy that followed, he frankly admitted that persistent legal challenges from defence attorneys could delay a final decision for as long as six years.

WANTED MAN

Meanwhile, the stance of the Mexican government regarding El Chapo's future had turned full circle. In 2014, when Guzmán was recaptured after more than a decade on the run, Attorney General Jesús Murillo Karam quipped that the prisoner would be extradited to the United States only after he had completed his jail sentence in accordance with Mexican law – 'in three or four hundred years!' But now the government of President Peña Nieto appeared keen to see the back of its most problematic citizen.

On Tuesday, 12 January 2016, Attorney General Arely Gómez flew to

Miami for the first face-to-face meeting with United States officials to discuss Guzmán's fate. US federal prosecutors already had cases open on Guzmán in Chicago, Miami and both Brooklyn and Manhattan in New York. So even if the bid for extradition were to be successful, there still remained the question of who would take responsibility for the prosecution. That decision would come down to the United States Attorney General, Lorretta Lynch.

In the first instance, El Chapo's defence attorneys were doing all they could to thwart extradition. In accordance with Mexican law, the defence team was allowed three days to present arguments against the move and 20 further days to provide the court with supporting documentation.

Juan Pablo Badillo, one of Guzmán's many lawyers, had already filed six *amparos*, motions challenging the extradition request. (*Amparos* literally means 'shelter' and it was devised as a guarantee that an individual's constitutional rights would be protected.) 'Our country must respect national sovereignty, the sovereignty of its institutions to impart justice,' he said with force.

But within two months, Guzmán himself would have a change of heart, a decision, it was claimed, that was a consequence of the poor conditions in Altiplano. Eduardo Guerreo, head of Mexico's prison system, had already described Guzmán's mental state as, 'depressed... more than depressed, tired – tired of being on the run'. His solution was to allow Guzmán some prison reading material: he was given a copy of Miguel de Cervantes' epic novel *Don Quixote* along with a self-help book called *The Purpose Driven Life: What on Earth Am I Here For?* by Californian evangelist Rick Warren.

Meanwhile, Guzmán's young beauty queen wife, Emma Coronel, broke silence, giving her first-ever public interview. Talking to broadcaster Telemundo, she described her husband as being 'slowly tortured' and said she was 'afraid for his life'. Since his recapture, Guzmán had been held in solitary confinement. 'They want to make him pay for his escape. They say that they are not punishing him. Of course, they are. They are there with him, watching him in his cell… They don't let him sleep. He has no privacy, not even to go to the bathroom.'

The credibility of her argument was perhaps stretched by her claims that she had had no idea about her husband's criminal activities. 'He's not violent, he's not rude, I've never seen him say a bad word to anyone.' She confirmed her stance as the loyal wife and mother by declaring: 'I'll follow him wherever because I am in love with him.'

On 2 March, Guzmán's attorney José Refugio Rodríguez told the newspaper *Reforma* that he had been instructed to broker a deal with the US authorities in exchange for better prison conditions in a less severe facility. 'He pleaded with me to look for the quickest way possible of processing extradition because he can no longer stand the situation he's experiencing.'

BUNKERED

It would hardly have surprised the aggrieved cartel leader that any privileges he might once have enjoyed were impossible after his recapture. Gone were the regular four-hour conjugal visits, the Viagra, the daily conferences with his lawyers and the hour he was allowed to spend each day out in the open air. He was now in permanent solitary confinement. This time the authorities were taking no chances. 'He's sleeping perfectly. There is no violation, I insist, of his fundamental rights,' security commissioner Renato Sales told Mexico's media, 'but shouldn't someone who twice escaped from maximum-security prisons be subject to special security measures? The common-sense answer is yes.'

While Guzmán awaited his fate, a controversial new side-story emerged when a California businesswoman revealed herself to be El Chapo's daughter. The 39-year-old Rosa Isela Guzmán Ortiz had lived in the United States for two decades and ran a chain of cafés and beauty salons. She had apparently been given permission by her father to speak to the British *Guardian* newspaper.

Incredibly, she claimed that the world's most wanted criminal had twice crossed the border to visit her while on the run. She painted a picture of Guzmán's world which would further embarrass the Mexican authorities. 'My dad is not a criminal. The government is guilty,' she said. He was, she claimed, a family man who had 'already retired... it was just a case of smoothing it over with El Mayo [Guzmán's partner Ismael Zambada]... we're completely sure El Mayo betrayed him.'

Yet she now seemed to be alleging that there had been a pact with some elements of the Mexican government which allowed her father to carry out his activities with little hindrance. Indeed, it was widely believed that both Mexican and US governments, while publicly claiming to be in pursuit of El Chapo, had been prepared to allow the Sinaloa cartel to dominate the drug-trafficking routes so long as it brought an end to the savage internecine violence.

But with changing administrations and shifts in power bases, Guzmán had now lost some of his leverage. He was now expendable. 'The government broke its promise,' Ortiz claimed. 'Now that they catch him, they say he's a criminal, a killer. But they didn't say that when they asked for money for their campaigns. They're hypocrites!'

The implication that El Chapo had given money to fund political campaigns was seized upon by Mexico's opposition parties. While hardly a revelation to anyone in the know about how the cartels operated, there were clearly questions to be answered. Elections were due in two years, and presidential candidate Andrés Manuel López Obrador – who would indeed win the 2018 election – demanded an official response: 'What El Chapo's daughter said is a strong revelation, which must be investigated and must be taken seriously. [President] Peña Nieto cannot stay silent.'

The National Action Party spokesman, Fernando Rodríguez Doval, told *Reforma*: 'A clear disavowal, an authentic clarification [is required] because it's a very sensitive issue... this matter of there being complicity on the part of prison authorities in the escape.'

A further twist emerged when Emma Coronel waded into the row, claiming that Rosa Isela Guzmán Ortiz was not her husband's daughter, and that his family had, 'never known of the existence of this person'. Ortiz was unrepentant, even agreeing to take a DNA test: 'I'm not going to deny anything at all,' she told reporters. 'I have a document which says I'm his daughter.' To back up her words, Ortiz was in possession of a birth certificate that named El Chapo as her father. 'All I know is that my dad told his lawyer to deliver some cheques to [a politician's] campaign, and asked that he respect him.'

The Mexican government engaged in its own damage limitation exercise as national security commissioner Renato Sales denied all allegations that Guzmán had bought protection from officials and politicians. 'Not treaties, nor alliances, nor pacts with [cartel] crime,' he said. 'We will not give in to speculation whose only objective is to divert attention [and] make this subject a victim.'

ON THE MOVE AGAIN

At the beginning of May, Guzmán was transferred from Altiplano to Cefereso No. 9, a federal penitentiary close to the border with El Paso at Ciudad Juárez. This was officially a part of the Mexico's National Security Commission's rotation policy aimed at preventing planned jailbreaks; as part of the same process, during his time there Guzmán would also be forced to change cells regularly.

The authorities were taking no chances. But local politicians saw El Chapo's presence in their territory as a sign of confidence. 'This speaks well of the state's [security] system, speaks very well of the environment that we are experiencing in Chihuahua, and above all, the strengthening of [our] institutions,' Governor César Duarte told *Reforma*. 'The security conditions are well above those in Altiplano, so there is no risk of an escape.' The move took Guzmán's legal team by surprise. They complained that they were given no advance warning and raised concerns for his welfare, especially as Cefereso No. 9 had been ranked by the Human Rights Commission as the worst of Mexico's already poorly regarded federal prisons.

Dressed as an angel and messenger of peace, a young man who is a member of the Psalm 100 Evangelical Church urges the family of El Chapo to give their lives to Jesus Christ outside Cefereso No. 9 penitentiary, where he was serving time.

Within days, two separate Mexican federal judges had ruled that Guzmán could be extradited to face charges lodged separately in Texas and California for conspiracy to import and distribute cocaine and marijuana, money laundering, arms possession and murder. Mexico's foreign ministry had 20 days to approve the extradition.

That decision was taken on 20 May 2016, the Mexican foreign ministry stated, after 'the US government provided sufficient assurances that the death penalty shall not apply if Mr Guzmán Loera were extradited and tried in that country'. Guzmán's legal team continued to lodge a number of appeals, and was successful in getting a stay of extradition after arguing that the statute of limitations on some of these crimes had now run out. But the final conclusion seemed inevitable. El Chapo Guzmán would be extradited in early 2017.

Prosecutors in the United States, meanwhile, began looking at ways of securing the easiest conviction, and took the decision to quietly drop the charges of murder against Guzmán; since these all took place in Mexico, the trial could have been derailed by disputes over the authority of the US courts to rule on crimes committed in a foreign country. In any case, his other crimes were – if he was convicted – sufficiently serious to see him locked away for the rest of his life.

In September 2014, a grand jury indictment against Guzmán had been filed in Brooklyn, New York, where the Sinaloa cartel was accused of trafficking four tonnes of cocaine in 2002. In May 2016, it was reported that Brooklyn had 'won' the right to try Guzmán over Chicago, San Diego and El Paso. Indeed, the Attorney General of the United States, Loretta Lynch, had lodged the original indictment when she was a federal prosecutor in Brooklyn. If there was to be a show trial for El Chapo, it was going to be in New York City. The media was already calling it 'The Trial of the Century'.

On 19 January 2017, a formal announcement was made. 'The government of the Republic announces that today the Fifth Appellate Criminal Court in Mexico City ruled to deny the protection of the Federal Justice system to Joaquín Guzmán Loera against the agreements made by the Ministry of Foreign Affairs on 20 May 2016, which permitted his extradition to the United States of America to be tried for various crimes, after finding that those agreements complied with constitutional requirements, the requirements of bilateral treaties and other legal rulings that are in effect and that his human rights were not, and have not been, violated by these proceedings.'

That same day, Guzmán was taken from his cell at the Cefereso No. 9 prison in Ciudad Juárez and handed over to members of the United States Drug Enforcement Agency. They boarded an aircraft for New York City, his eventual destination being the maximum-security wing of the Metropolitan Correctional Center in Lower Manhattan.

Guzmán's arrival in the United States was characterized in some quarters as a 'peace offering' to America's newly elected leader, Donald Trump, who was to be sworn in as president the following day. Throughout his year-long campaign to reach the pinnacle of American politics, Trump had often been disparaging about Mexico and its illegal immigrants. 'They are not our friend, believe me… They're bringing drugs. They're bringing crime. They're rapists. And some, I assume, are good people.'

If elected, Trump claimed he would sanction the building of a wall along the 2,000-mile (3,200-km) southern border. And that Mexico would pay for it. ('I'm not paying for that fucking wall!' Mexico's president Vicente Fox exclaimed in February 2016.) All the while, Trump rallies would inevitably erupt into massed chants of 'Build The Wall! Build The Wall!'

Mexico's attorney general's office insisted it had nothing to do with Trump's inauguration. 'Under the terms of the international treaty, we were obliged to immediately do the handover of a person requested by the United States government,' Alberto Elías Beltrán told *Reforma*. But there could be little question that it eased an increasingly thorny relationship between the two countries. The US authorities were said to have been surprised by the specific timing. 'The [US] justice department extends its gratitude to the government of Mexico for their extensive cooperation and assistance in securing the extradition of Guzmán Loera to the United States,' read an official statement.

An initial brief hearing took place at Brooklyn federal court the day following Guzmán's arrival in the United States. Clean-shaven and dressed in a standard dark-blue prison smock, T-shirt and tennis shoes, Guzmán – who appeared to have gained a good deal of weight since his recapture – was read the charges against him.

Speaking through a translator, he acknowledged that he understood them, pleaded not guilty to all charges and declined to apply for bail. Acting US Attorney General Sally Yates, announcing the charges, described Guzmán as 'the alleged leader of a multi-billion-dollar, multi-national criminal enterprise that funnelled drugs onto our streets and violence and misery into our communities'. Robert Capers, the United States attorney for the Eastern District of New York, introduced the 17-count indictment. 'Guzmán's story is not one of a do-gooder, or a Robin Hood, or an escape artist,' he said. 'Guzmán's rise was akin to that of a small cancerous tumour that metastasized into a full-blown scourge that for decades littered the streets of Mexico with the casualties of violent drug wars... [and] helped to perpetrate the drug epidemic here in the US.'

A 56-page memo outlined the prosecution's approach to the trial, centred around 'a large coterie of cooperating witnesses', including many who claimed to have had personal dealings with Guzmán and the Sinaloa cartel. Other witnesses would testify to 'specific murders carried out under Guzmán's orders', the mass bribery of Mexican politicians and law-enforcement officials, and proof that came in the form of accounts ledgers, intercepted cellphone calls and text messages. US District Judge Brian Cogan scheduled the trial to begin on 5 September 2018; it was later postponed two months to 5 November 2018.

UNFAIR TREATMENT?

During the 22 months before the trial was due to begin, Guzmán's lawyers once again made public claims about the conditions under which he was being held. At a court hearing on 3 February attended by his wife Emma Coronel, they stated that the restrictions he was living under made it difficult for them to make decisions relating to the defence; he had even been refused a glass of water during a three-hour legal meeting. Judge Cogan was unrepentant: 'Based on what I know about this case, there are grounds for extra security measures.'

A month later, the situation further escalated when Amnesty International declared themselves 'concerned that the conditions imposed on [Guzmán] appear to be unnecessarily harsh and to breach international standards for humane treatment'. Public defence attorney Michelle Gelernt weighed in. 'Mr Guzmán is being held under the worst, most restrictive conditions of any prisoner currently detained by the United States government,' she declared. 'Even convicted prisoners held in the notorious federal Supermax in Colorado are allowed to watch television in their cells, exercise outside where they can speak with other inmates, and speak with their families. Mr Guzmán enjoys none of these benefits.'

Similar complaints kept arising in the months leading up to the trial. Guzmán's defence team was led by a well-known New York lawyer named Jeffrey Lichtman. Eight years earlier, he had made his name successfully defending John Gotti Jr., boss of the Gambino crime family, but he knew the task he now faced would be tougher still. He too questioned the conditions under which his client was being kept. 'He's in isolation 24 hours a day and his condition is deteriorating,' he reported. 'He has no contact with other prisoners and very little contact with jailers – who don't speak Spanish. He has no ability to speak to his family and gets two calls from his sister totalling half-an-hour a month.'

Lichtman weighed in on the background to the trial. It was, he said, 'Literally an inquisition… Constitutional fairness has gone out of the window because the government wants a show trial with a quickie conviction.' He launched an early punch at the opposition when he lambasted the mounds of evidence that the prosecutors were claiming to have amassed. 'It's making me think that maybe the evidence is not so good and they're going to rely on the evidence of people who've spent their entire lives selling drugs and lying,' he said.

The lead prosecutor was to be Andrea Goldbarg, a former deputy district attorney for Brooklyn who had plenty of experience of cartel drug trials. She had previously worked on the prosecution of Alfredo Beltrán Leyva – a former close ally who became a bitter enemy of the Sinaloa cartel – securing him a conviction of life in prison for drug-trafficking in 2017.

Under the most extreme security measures ever seen at the United States District Court for the Eastern District of New York in Brooklyn, the federal criminal court case of *United States of America vs. Joaquín Guzmán Loera* got under way on 5 November 2018. The building was patrolled by armed guards with sniffer dogs and everyone entering the court had to pass through a metal detector. The Brooklyn Bridge was temporarily closed while Guzmán was transported from his cell; to reduce traffic disruption, Guzmán was later held at an undisclosed location for the duration of the trial.

It had already been agreed that the identities of the jurors would remain secret. After two-and-half days of interviews by Judge Cogan and the lawyers, 12 jurors were selected to decide the outcome of the case – 8 women and 4 men. Beforehand, they were questioned on whether they knew anything about Guzmán, whether they had searched him online or watched any of the many TV shows and documentaries about him.

All but one said they were familiar with him. A number of jurors were recused: one had 'definite views on the case', another – a Michael Jackson impersonator – claimed to be 'too well-known', while a third admitted to being 'a bit of a fan' of El Chapo, which drew a smile from Guzmán when told this by his translator.

THE TRIAL BEGINS

The first of the opening statements was made on Tuesday 13 November 2018. Guzmán entered the courtroom at 9:30am wearing a dark-blue suit and tie. Already seated, as she would be throughout the trial, was the immaculately dressed Emma Coronel. Guzmán attempted to approach his wife but was prevented from doing so by court marshals.

Hoping to simplify the trial, the prosecution had by this time reduced the indictment count from 17 to 10, removing, among other items, the charges for murder, which they knew would be harder to prove. In its opening statement, the prosecution reiterated that Guzmán had been the leader of the world's most powerful drug cartel from 1989 to 2014, and that the Sinaloa cartel had trafficked cocaine and other drugs into the United States worth up to $10 million (£8m) a day. 'Money. Drugs. Murder. A vast, global narcotics-trafficking empire. That's what this case is about, and that's what the evidence will show,' claimed prosecutor Adam Fels.

The government's case, it was clear, would rest on the testimony of its witnesses, many of whom were convicted criminals now under US government protection programmes, some of whom had been offered reduced sentences in return for their court appearances.

Jeffrey Lichtman gave a characteristically provocative response for the defence. The prosecution, he claimed, was 'focusing on the mythical El Chapo figure'. Instead, he portrayed Guzmán as a scapegoat, a fall-guy for the true head of the Sinaloa cartel, 'a man who has never been to jail', Ismael El Mayo Zambada. 'There is another side to this story,' he began. 'An uglier side. It's a side the governments of Mexico and the United States don't want you to hear... This is a case which will require you to open your minds to the possibility that government officials at the very highest level can be bribed, can conspire to commit horrible crimes – that American law-enforcement agents can also be crooked.' He then turned his attention to the prosecution's witnesses. 'Imagine witnesses who have lied every single day of their lives since they could walk,' he said. 'Witnesses who have killed prosecutors, who have tried to kill presidents of other countries – that's who give life to the government's case. People who will make your skin crawl when they testify here.'

Lichtman's barnstorming opening drew criticism from two former Mexican presidents: a spokesman for Enrique Peña Nieto called the allegations 'false and defamatory'; his predecessor Felipe Calderón went on social media, tweeting that the remarks were 'absolutely false and reckless'. The federal prosecution was outraged, demanding the statement be thrown out. Judge Cogan let it stand, but admonished Lichtman as having travelled 'far afield of direct or circumstantial proof'. The jury, he said, would be instructed to focus only on the evidence presented to them.

The prosecution raised eyebrows on Wednesday 15 November by calling one of their key witnesses so early in the case. Jesús Zambada García had been the Sinaloa cartel's chief accountant – one of what he called its 'sub-leaders' for more than a decade. He confirmed to the court

Jeffrey Lichtman, attorney for El Chapo Guzmán, arrives at the US Federal Courthouse in Brooklyn, February 2019.

that El Chapo Guzmán and his brother El Mayo Zambada were the two main figures in the cartel.

Establishing his links to Guzmán, he claimed to have organized helicopter transport for him after his 2001 jailbreak. Zambada described the structure of the cartel, the way it operated, the hit men (the *sicarios*) and the ease with which politicians and government officials could be bribed. He also illustrated how such vast personal wealth was accrued, with cartel leaders combining their personal fortunes to buy shipments of cocaine directly from Colombia. He had the figures to hand. Profitability per kilogram was in the range of $13–26,000 (£10,500–21,000), meaning that the cartel could make around $450 million (£363m) from a single shipment – and that 15 to 20 per cent of that profit would go to a single investor. The numbers were mind-boggling, so much so that Zambada was unable to answer how much these shipments were worth in a typical year. 'Billions,' came the reply, most of which would be 'invested in other shipments'.

The following day, much of Zambada's testimony focused on the bribery of high-ranking police and military officials. He told the court that Guzmán had once instructed him to give $100,000 (£80,000) 'and a hug' to a general for reasons he claimed were 'unspecified'. He also told the court that the Sinaloa's highest-ranking government official, Genaro García Luna, architect of Mexico's War on Drugs, was paid two instalments of $3 million (£2.42m) in cash-filled suitcases, once while leading the federal investigation agency, and again after he had been appointed minister for public security.

He further alleged that García Luna had been paid $56 million (£45m) on El Chapo's behalf by the Beltrán Leyva brothers – then allies of the Sinaloa – who specialized in bribing corrupt officials. (A year after the trial, García Luna was arrested in Dallas, Texas, unable to explain his vast personal wealth. The former US Ambassador to Mexico, Roberta S. Jacobson, maintained that the Calderón administration was well aware of the links between Luna and the Sinaloa cartel.)

As Zambada left the courtroom on the final day of his evidence, he nodded to his former friend; El Chapo rolled his eyes to the ceiling in acknowledgement.

THE 'DEGENERATES' BEGIN TO TALK

During the weeks that followed, the prosecution continued its relentless onslaught of witnesses, some of whom had few direct links with Guzmán himself, but whose testimony nonetheless added to the 'bulk' of evidence stacking up against him. For those in the courtroom, the trial would frequently drag under the sheer weight of questionable detail.

Media attention was once again piqued on 27 November, when another significant figure from the Sinaloa was brought to the stand. Security measures were even tighter than usual before the arrival of Miguel Ángel Martínez, a man who had survived numerous attempts on his life while in prison and who was now said to be living under a US witness protection programme. Courtroom artists were instructed not even to sketch his face.

Known as 'El Gordo' (The Fat One), Martínez reported directly to Guzmán himself – unlike Zambada, who worked for his brother El Mayo – and had been one of his most trusted lieutenants. His testimony shed extraordinary detail on the trafficking methods used by the Sinaloa and the wealth and lifestyle of its leader.

Vast quantities of illegal merchandise, he told the court, were moved into the United States, often through a network of cross-border tunnels. This was already known to authorities – they had discovered an unfinished, solar-powered tunnel stretching from Jacumé, Baja, south of the border, into California; this was equipped with lighting, ventilation, water pumps and a rail system. Tanker trucks with secret compartments and even fake chilli pepper cans were all used to hide drugs while they were being transported. For the return journey to Mexico, they would be loaded with tens of millions of dollars in cash; Guzmán, he claimed, would send three private planes to Tijuana each month to collect the money. It would be stored in Samsonite cases in safe houses until bank officials could be bribed to change it for Mexican pesos.

Martínez went on to detail incidents that could have come straight out of a TV narco-drama, including the codewords used for traffickers over the radio to avoid detection. When Guzmán wanted aircraft prepared for a shipment, he told his lieutenants he was 'throwing a party'; jet fuel was 'wine' and the planes were 'girls'.

Such was El Chapo's wealth, Martínez claimed, that he owned a $10 million (£8m) Acapulco beach house with its own private zoo complete with roaming lions, tigers and panthers and a miniature train from which to view the animals. There was also his luxury yacht, 'Chapito', and, he continued, 'four to five women' that he 'maintained'. But he could also be generous to those he trusted, lavishing gifts of diamond-studded watches and luxury cars on them.

Cross-examining for the defence, Jeffrey Lichtman told the court that Martínez's testimony should be dismissed since he'd had a severe cocaine addiction during the time he worked for Guzmán – indeed, he admitted that at its peak he had been using up to four grams of the drug each day. Lichtman referred to most of the prosecution witnesses as 'degenerates' – as far as he was concerned, Miguel Ángel Martínez was no exception.

THE 'DRUGS' TRAIN

Another former associate provided fascinating evidence against Guzmán on 10 December. Tirso Martinez Sancho claimed to be responsible for overseeing 'the drugs train' that ran cocaine from Mexico City to New York City. Tankers would transport cooking oil into Mexico; the oil would be siphoned out and hidden compartments would be stacked with kilos of cocaine. A layer of oil was left at the bottom of the tank to deter customs officials from crawling in for too close an inspection. The trains would pull into a warehouse in New Jersey and the cargo was emptied into box trucks that took the cocaine to warehouses in New York City.

Following the holiday break, the trial resumed on Thursday 3 January 2019 with a prosecution witness that surprised many. Vicente Zambada Niebla was not only the son of Guzmán's partner El Mayo Zambada, but had been seen by many as an eventual heir apparent, groomed to take over from El Chapo himself. Yet now he was set to give evidence against his former boss.

Extradited to the United States in 2010, he was due to face trial in March 2019 but agreed a plea-bargain arrangement with the US court in Illinois on condition that he testified against Guzmán. 'El Vincentillo' had worked with his father since he was a child, in effect growing up within the Sinaloa cartel. 'Little by little I started getting involved in my father's business,' he said. 'By 2001, I was a more important person in the cartel… another boss.'

Vicente Zambada Niebla, 'El Vicentillo', photographed at the time of his capture in Mexico in 2009.

By this time, he was the cartel's operations and logistics manager. And by his own admission, he oversaw the import of cocaine from Colombia to Mexico and its journey onward to Los Angeles and Chicago. Shockingly, he described a meeting he organized with executives at Pemex, Mexico's state-owned oil company, to discuss transporting cocaine in one of its tankers.

Throughout his two days of testimony, Zambada referred to Guzmán politely as 'my *compadre* Chapo' and gave first-hand evidence of the inner workings of the Sinaloa under Guzmán and his father. He further claimed to have worked as a spy for the Drugs Enforcement Agency, trading information on rivals of the Sinaloa to the US authorities.

There was a common belief that it was El Vincentillo's father, El Mayo Zambada, who had betrayed Guzmán to take sole control of the Sinaloa cartel, and that this testimony was all part of a broader plan to take down El Chapo once and for all – and at the same time secure reduced sentences for his son and brother. There could be little doubt, though, that the central thrust of the defence argument, that Guzmán was merely a 'middle manager [who] had to take orders from someone else', was by this time dead in the water.

THE SOUND-PROOFED HOUSE OF DEATH

As the procession of witnesses continued, a low-ranking cartel trafficker was introduced by the prosecutors. Edgar Ivan Galván from El Paso, Texas was arrested in 2011 and hoped to get a reduction on his 24-year jail term by giving evidence. Guzmán and Galván were at opposite ends of the business and, unsurprisingly, had never come into contact with one another. Yet he was able to shed fascinating light on his extremely unglamorous life as a foot soldier within the cartel.

The former taxi driver had fallen on hard times after his divorce until he met Antonio 'Jaguar' Marrufo, a brutally violent Sinaloa hitman, at a party. Galván ended up working for Marrufo, smuggling AK-47 rifles from Texas into Ciudad Juárez, and then returning to the United States with cocaine. Marrufo had boasted to Galván about his extensive 'cleaning' work on behalf of El Chapo as he sought to gain control of the Juárez border crossings.

On one occasion, Galván was taken to a sound-proofed house in Juárez with a white-tiled floor sloping towards a drain. In this house, Marrufo said, 'No noise came out if someone was to scream. That's where he killed people.'

Galván's testimony gave credence to claims made earlier by Vicente Zambada, that almost all of the Mexican drug cartels' vast armouries – rifles, rocket and grenade-launchers, stinger anti-aircraft missiles, armoured vehicles – came from the United States into Mexico, where it's illegal to purchase guns. The truth behind what has been called the 'iron river', which continues to fuel Mexico's drug violence, is that most of these weapons were bought legally over the counter in America and smuggled across the border.

In the 1990s, Juan García Abrego, head of the Juárez cartel, was known to have bought seven gunshops in Brownsville, Texas which he used to run weaponry across the border. The United States Bureau of Alcohol, Tobacco, Firearms and Explosives (ATF) have reported that intermediaries are paid up to $100 (£80) a time to make untraceable purchases. 'We have seen them use the little old guy on the park bench, or homeless people... to buy guns on their behalf,' said ATF agent William Newell. 'We are at a crossroads where firearms trafficking and the drug trade come together,' his colleague Tom Mangan agreed. 'It really is the perfect storm.'

In the week that followed, the prosecution changed tack, presenting intercepted text messages and wire-tapped cellphone calls to the court. An unassuming man named Cristian Rodríguez had been a technical consultant for Guzmán between 2008 and 2012, employed to install FlexiSPY security software on an estimated 50 cartel phones, so that he could track and monitor texts and conversations without the user's knowledge.

Rodríguez's work had been referenced by other witnesses earlier in the trial, but what they hadn't known was that in 2010 he had been recruited by FBI special agent Steven Marston. Posing as a Russian gangster, Marston persuaded Rodríguez to allow him access to communications codes used on the VOIP (Voice Over the Internet Protocol) servers that ran in the Netherlands. Rodríguez told the court that Guzmán had become obsessed with the technology and instructed him to install it on computers as well as cellphones. He was even able to listen remotely to conversations.

Rodríguez recalled: 'He would call a person to their extension, they would talk, they would hang up, and then he would call another line to open the microphone and listen to what was being said about him.'

Guzmán was especially keen to keep his many romantic sidelines under wraps. 'He was with a woman, and the woman had a computer in the house,' Rodríguez recalled. 'He asked me how long it would take me to make the computer "special".' Rodríguez explained that it would take just three minutes; Guzmán distracted the woman while the software was installed.

MUNDANE CHIT-CHAT

Marston turned up to present some of the intercepted messages to the court; not only did they provide a unique glimpse into the everyday life of Guzmán and the Sinaloa cartel, but they also suggested that Guzmán's wife, Emma Coronel, had greater knowledge of his criminal life than she had claimed. They nevertheless indicated genuine affection between El Chapo and Coronel; the messages were sometimes flirtatious, sometimes intimate. He would refer to her as 'Reinita Coronel' – his 'Little Queen' – or simply 'RC'.

Much of the content comprised the kind of mundane chit-chat familiar to most married couples, albeit those with unlimited wealth: Coronel was unhappy with a $12,000 (£9,500) watch he had bought her and wanted to return it. They discussed shopping – he asked her to buy him underwear, shirts and sneakers; asked if there was anything else he needed, he replied: 'Black moustache dye'.

They also showed a hitherto unseen side of El Chapo, that of the doting father, as they discussed their twin daughters, Mali and Kiki, then 18 months old. He even made a joke about arming them. 'Our Kiki is fearless. I'm going to give her an AK-47 so she can hang with me!' (Shortly before the trial broke up for the holiday period, his daughters, now seven years old, were brought into court by their mother – to the visible delight of both them and their father.)

HUMILIATION

The proceedings took an uncomfortable turn for Guzmán, however, when romantic exchanges with one of his mistresses, Agustina Cabanillas Acosta, were read out to the courtroom. Guzmán evidently enjoyed a very close relationship with Cabanillas, referring to her as 'Fiera' ('wild beast').

The wife of El Chapo, Emma Coronel Aispuro (left), listens as attorney Michelle Gelernt answers questions from reporters outside the US Federal Courthouse.

It was clear that she played an active role within the cartel, since so much of their communication was about business. In one exchange, they discussed buying 700 tons (680 tonnes) of cocaine in Belize. On another occasion, they mentioned forming new companies, including a chemical fertilizer business in Germany which could be used to export drugs to 'Europe, Canada and Australia'. In their texts, they addressed each other as 'love', Guzmán telling her: 'I adore you; you are the most important person to me.'

During all this time, Emma Coronel sat stone-faced in the gallery, the knowing intimate glances and blown kisses the couple had shared throughout the trial now noticeably absent; when the court went into recess, some observers claimed that she could not even look at him.

Guzmán's humiliation was by no means over, though. Even throughout a trial that looked set to see him jailed for the remainder of his life, he had managed to maintain an upbeat air; he now sat sullen as intercepted messages from his mistress were played to the courtroom.

Discussing El Chapo with a friend, Coronel confided: 'I'm going to play along to see what else this idiot tells me… I don't trust these BlackBerries, the ones he gives me over here, because the bastard can locate me.'

SINISTER UNDERTONE

Other evidence indicated the risks of being intimately involved with El Chapo. Lucero Guadalupe Sánchez López was a local Sinaloa politician for three years before her 2017 arrest on drug-trafficking charges while attempting to cross the border. She and Guzmán had begun an affair in 2011 and she is also thought to have given birth to his son. Testifying against her former lover as part of a plea bargain, she discussed a number of romantic text messages, some of which had a sinister undertone.

Realizing their illicit affair was in danger of coming out into the open, Guzmán messaged her: 'Look, the Mafia kills people who don't pay or people who snitch, but not if you're serious, love… Lies are what cause problems. Don't lie and people will always see the good, love.

Always remember that. I'm telling you this because I love you.' Sánchez responded that she was not doing anything wrong and reiterated how much she loved him.

But in court on 17 January she admitted to being terrified that 'he could actually hurt me'. She went on to recall an incident where Guzmán's secretary interrupted one of their trysts to tell him that an associate was dead. To her, the meaning was clear enough. 'He turned around and looked at me in a slow demeanour... He said from that point on, whoever betrayed him, they would die. Whether they were family or women, they were going to die.'

In court, Sánchez, known by the local media in Sinaloa as 'Chapodiputada' (Deputy Chapo), described being in bed with Guzmán during a police raid on a Culiacán safe house in February 2014, two days before his arrest. A naked El Chapo directed her to the bathroom where he pressed a button that raised the bathtub, revealing an escape tunnel. To Emma Coronel's apparent amusement, Sanchez wept in court as she told the jury: 'I thought we were in a romantic relationship.'

A seemingly endless procession of prosecution witnesses, all with damning accounts of Guzmán's activities, threatened to overwhelm the trial at times. Indeed, Judge Brian Cogan was forced to have words with one of the jurors who would periodically doze off during proceedings.

The tales of violence, bribery and corruption continued apace. The court heard claims of further inducements paid to an advisor of the current Mexican president, Ándres Manuel López Obrador, during his unsuccessful 2006 campaign. Convicted Colombian narco Alex Cifuentes Villa made the shocking suggestion that former president Enrique Peño Nieto had approached the wanted El Chapo, proposing that a payment of $250 million (£200m) would put an end to the manhunt. Both politicians, unsurprisingly, made robust public denials of the allegations.

On 23 January, another of Guzmán's top lieutenants was called to the stand. Dámasco López Núñez, known as 'El Licenciado' (The Graduate) because of his law degree, told the jury that Emma Coronel played a central role in the infamous 2015 jailbreak. 'She was giving us orders,' he recalled. She had also organized the purchase of the property adjacent to the prison that enabled the 1 mile/1.6 km-long escape tunnel to be built.

BURIED ALIVE

A day later, former bodyguard Isaías Valdez Ríos provided a chilling description of how Guzmán had tortured and then murdered at least three members of rival cartels. He told the court how one prisoner was left outside for three days and then interrogated by Guzmán, who afterwards shot him in cold blood, and while he was still gasping for breath ordered his men to dump him in a grave and bury him alive.

Guzmán seemed to reserve particular brutality for those who came from his home state but worked for the Los Zetas cartel. He had his men torture the victims before he beat them himself. 'The people were pretty much like rag dolls. The bones in their bodies were fractured. They couldn't move,' Valdez told the court. The bodies were then burned, with Guzmán telling his men: 'I don't want any bones left over.'

During the testimony, the jury was shown gruesome TV footage of the aftermath of a Sinaloa cartel attack, the grim details narrated by Valdez himself. The film, shot in 2009, showed bullet-riddled cars, shattered glass and blood-soaked upholstery. (The court was spared the images of corpses and dismembered arms and legs that had also been recorded.)

Valdez and his colleagues had been on their way to a party when they received instructions from Guzmán to make a hit on a rival. What began as a stake-out to assassinate a single gunman turned into a 20-minute bloodbath that left 'seven or eight' enemies dead.

In fact, Valdez wound up on the wrong end of El Chapo's ire. Given $250,000 (£200,000) to buy airstrips in Honduras, Valdez was rumoured to have absconded with the money, spending it on houses, cars and Rolexes – a claim he denied. 'I was scared, I hid, I turned off all communication,' he said.

In the end, he managed to convince the gunman sent to kill him that the accusations were lies. Guzmán later called him, accepting his word. Ríos also told the court how El Chapo was often gifted specially made guns by admirers or those hoping to win his favour. The jury were shown photographs of Guzmán's diamond-studded handguns, and told of a particular favourite, a gold-plated AK-47 rife.

'NO LAUGHING'

On 28 January, which turned out to be the final day of the prosecution's presentation, proceedings briefly took on a surreal air when Mexican actor Alejandro Edda, who played El Chapo in the popular Netflix series *Narcos*, made a surprise appearance in the gallery of the Brooklyn courtroom. He was said to be researching scenes that he would doubtless soon be filming himself, and throughout the day he scribbled copiously in his notebook. On arrival, the actor greeted Emma Coronel and they had a brief friendly exchange in Spanish. Alerted to Edda's presence by defence attorney William Purpura, the real-life El Chapo greeted him with a smile. 'He seemed happy,' Purpura confirmed. A US Marshall was less impressed with the display of levity, saying: 'No hand gestures, no thumbs-up. This isn't Comedy Central. No laughing.'

Throughout the trial there had been much speculation as to whether Guzmán would be called to the stand in his own defence. The government had spent the past 11 weeks presenting a grand total of 56 witnesses, who gave endless examples of El Chapo's crimes.

If only a tiny fraction of what had been reported was true, then Guzmán would spend the rest of his life behind bars. The jury heard the tales of a man who ran his drug-trafficking business with the ruthless efficiency of the president of a Fortune 500 corporation. It heard of the opulent lifestyle befitting a man on the *Forbes* billionaires list. It heard of his insatiable appetite for young women – one that, it could be argued, might have hastened his downfall.

El Chapo came in many different guises. There was the family man who doted on his wife and children. There was the man who spent billions bribing politicians and officials at every level of Mexican life. And there was the brutal murderer. What possible defence could there be?

As it happened, Guzmán did not speak. On Tuesday 29 January, his attorney, Jeffrey Lichtman, spent a grand total of 30 minutes questioning FBI agent Paul Roberts, Jr. about the testimonies of two of the prosecution witnesses, the Cifuentes brothers. The case for the defence was rested.

MOUNTAIN OF EVIDENCE AGAINST THE EMPIRE OF CRIME

Lead prosecutor Andrea Goldbarg began her closing statements the following day. The United States had presented, she said 'a mountain of evidence' against El Chapo Guzmán. Standing before a table full of AK-47 rifles and bricks of seized cocaine, she used a montage of images and intercepted audio to summarize the case. 'You heard it from his own words,' she told the jurors. 'This is the defendant running his empire… This is how he built his empire and protected it.'

She finally addressed what was sure to be at the centre of the defence's argument. 'Ladies and gentlemen, these witnesses are criminals. The government is not asking you to like them [but they] are testifying truthfully,' she told the jury. '[Guzmán is] guilty and he never wanted to be in a position where he'd have to answer to his crimes. Do not let him escape responsibility. Hold him accountable for his crimes.'

Summing up for the defence, Jeffrey Lichtman pointed out the '600lb gorilla in the room: reasonable doubt'. If there really was reasonable doubt, then a verdict of not guilty had to be brought. He launched an immediate attack on the witnesses and the plea bargains that had brought them there to testify. 'These witnesses lie, steal, cheat, deal drugs and kill people,' he told the jury. 'These witnesses [were] not only… lying every day of their lives – *of their miserable, selfish lives*,' he fumed, '"but they lied in this courtroom.'

Lichtman's argument remained that Guzmán was merely a scapegoat in a wide-ranging government conspiracy, and that the true head of the Sinaloa cartel, Ismael El Mayo Zambada, was – and remained – a free man.

'If you don't believe the co-operators who've testified against him,' he concluded, 'then you can't convict Mr. Guzmán.'

With the jury due to begin their deliberations three days later on Monday 4 February, sealed documents containing witness testimonies were made public following deputations by the *New York Times* and *Vice News*. These were not admissible as evidence in court since they were not directly connected to the charges Guzmán faced – and nor were the members of jury permitted access to their contents.

They nevertheless contained disturbing allegations. Guzmán's former secretary, Alex Cifuentes Villa, claimed that his boss had raped his mistress, Lucero Sánchez López, and had frequently had sexual relations with girls as young as 13 years old, which he referred to as his 'vitamins'.

'For approximately $5,000 (£4,000),' the document read, 'the defendant or one of his associates could have the girl of his choice brought to one of the defendant's ranches for sexual intercourse.' Cifuentes claimed to have assisted Guzmán by 'drugging the girls with whom [he] intended to have sex by placing a powdery substance into their drinks at the defendant's direction'.

These remain allegations for which Guzmán has never been charged. Furthermore, in her already damning witness testimony, Sánchez certainly never raised the matter as part of the evidence. Attorney Eduardo Balarezo, from Guzmán's defence team, offered a dismissive statement:'The government recently publicly filed documents containing extremely salacious information. Joaquín denies the allegations, which lack any corroboration and were deemed too prejudicial and unreliable to be admitted at trial. It is unfortunate that the material was publicly released just prior to the jury beginning deliberations.'

THE TOTTING-UP PROCESS

At 1pm on Monday 4 February, the partly sequestered and anonymous jurors gathered. With the mountain of evidence against Guzmán, the prosecutors had expected a very quick decision to be made. Instead, they were surprised that within two hours they had requested clarifications on technicalities relating to firearms and drug descriptions. But faced with an eight-page verdict sheet there was to be no immediate decision.

After five days with no decision, the jury retired for the weekend. This was good news for Guzmán and his team. With a broad grin, the defendant laughed and bear-hugged his attorney Jeffrey Lichtman; for the first time, the government prosecutors began to exhibit nerves.

With little to report on the trial, the media turned its attention to El Chapo's family. Holed up at the boutique Tillary Hotel in Brooklyn, Emma Coronel took to Instagram, where she began her own personal defence. Referring to her being 'exposed in doubt' during the trial, she continued: 'I can only say that I have nothing to be ashamed of. I am not perfect, but I consider myself a good human being who has never hurt anyone intentionally.'

With all the publicity surrounding the case, she began to fear for her safety and hired a team of bodyguards. Meanwhile, Guzmán's daughter Alejandrina Gisselle had not been idle. In 2016, she had tried – and failed – to cash in on her father's celebrity by registering 'El Chapo' and 'El Chapo Guzmán' as trademarks. She now revealed her new business brand, 'El Chapo 701', selling clothing, footwear, jewellery and liquor. The website described the brand's inspiration as 'a humble seller of oranges with many goals and a great ambition'.

THE VERDICT

On its sixth day of deliberation, on 12 February 2019, the jury announced that it had reached its decision. Dressed in a black suit, grey shirt and black tie, El Chapo Guzmán awaited news of his fate.

It duly arrived, as follows:

Count 1: Engaging in a Continuing Criminal Enterprise
Guilty

Count 2: International Cocaine, Heroin, Methamphetamine and
  Marijuana Manufacture and Distribution Conspiracy
Guilty
Count 3: Cocaine Importation Conspiracy
Guilty
Count 4: Cocaine Distribution Conspiracy
Guilty
Count 5: International Distribution of Cocaine
Guilty
Count 6: International Distribution of Cocaine
Guilty
Count 7: International Distribution of Cocaine
Guilty
Count 8: International Distribution of Cocaine
Guilty
Count 9: Use of Firearms
Guilty
Count 10: Conspiracy to Launder Narcotics Proceeds
Guilty

Joaquín Archivaldo Guzmán Loera showed no emotion as the verdict on
each count was read out in the courtroom.

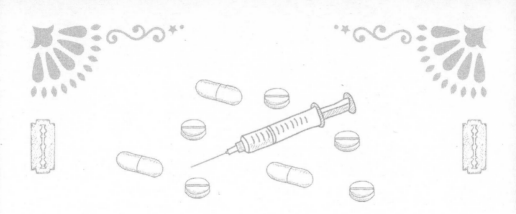

CHAPTER 8:
THE END OF THE ROAD

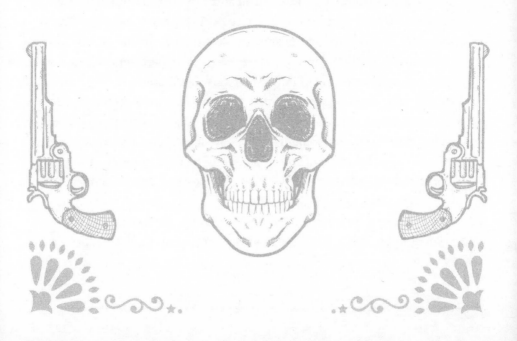

During the trial of *United States of America vs. Joaquín Guzmán Loera,* Brooklyn's federal courthouse – the United States District Court for the Eastern District of New York – had become a virtual fortress. Nothing was being left to chance: rooftop snipers, bomb-sniffing dogs, armed law-enforcement officers were all brought in to ensure that justice was seen to be done.

The National Guard, too, was out in force, with some officers even equipped with Geiger counters to detect possible radiation. The sensational media coverage guaranteed a growing stream of voyeurs who lined up outside the courtroom early each morning hoping to snatch a glimpse of the world's most famous 'narco don'.

By the final days of the trial, reporters and members of the public were regularly braving the freezing New York City winter temperatures, arriving ever earlier each night with their sleeping bags as they took their places outside the courtroom. Earlier in the trial, queues had begun to form around 6am, but now anyone arriving after 2am would find it almost impossible to get a place inside.

After six days of deliberation by the jury of seven women and five men, presiding Judge Brian M. Cogan read out their verdict on 12 February

2019: Joaquín Guzmán 'El Chapo' Loera was declared guilty on all counts. At the request of the defence team, Judge Cogan then questioned each juror individually, asking if this verdict was a reflection of their own vote; each replied that it was.

This had been a demanding case for a civilian jury. It had included 200 hours of testimony from 56 witnesses, including harrowing accounts from 14 of Guzmán's convicted former associates, all of whom had agreed to testify in exchange for a reduction in their own sentences.

And during that time Guzmán himself had remained silent – the only words he spoke were at the start of the trial when, through a Spanish interpreter, he indicated his own refusal to testify. Judge Cogan thanked the jury for their meticulous efforts throughout the trial: 'In my 13 years as a judge, I have never seen a jury pay this kind of attention to detail,' he noted. 'The way you went about it was really quite remarkable and frankly it made me proud to be an American.'

A motorcade takes El Chapo back into detention in Manhattan after attending a hearing at the US Federal Courthouse.

The first of the indictments against Guzmán, 'continuing criminal enterprise', was by far the most wide-ranging, consisting of 27 separate serious violations, among them conspiracy to traffic drugs and conspiracy to commit murder. He was pronounced guilty on 25 of the 27 violations within the count. Guzmán, who had pleaded not guilty to all charges, seemed visibly shaken by the verdict. His legal team would undoubtedly have made him aware that such an outcome on this count alone would result in an inevitably heavy sentence – mandatory life imprisonment without parole.

The sentencing was scheduled for four months later, tentatively estimated for 25 June. With a look of resignation, Guzmán smiled at his young wife, Emma Coronel Aispuro, who was seated – as she had been throughout the trial – in the second row of the gallery; both put hands to their hearts and made the thumbs-up gesture to one another. Guzmán was led away by two United States marshals, leaving his wife in tears.

IMPOSSIBLE ODDS

Outside the courtroom Guzmán's defence attorney, Jeffrey Lichtman, declared that his team was disappointed with the verdict but nevertheless respected the jury's decision. He told reporters about the impossible odds they were up against in defending a figure of Guzmán's notoriety: 'We were faced with extraordinary and unprecedented obstacles in defending Joaquín, including his detention in solitary confinement.'

Although 'devastated' by the outcome, Lichtman pledged nevertheless to appeal the verdict. 'Joaquín Guzmán, I understand what society thinks of him,' he concluded, 'but it was an absolute honour to represent him.' The case wasn't over. They would, he proclaimed, 'fight until our last breath'.

US Attorney Richard P. Donoghue held a press conference immediately afterwards. He declared the outcome a victory both for the United States and for Mexico. 'Today, Guzmán Loera has been held accountable for the tons of illegal narcotics he trafficked for more than two decades, the murders he ordered and committed, and the billions of dollars he reaped while causing incalculable pain and suffering to those devastated by his drugs… There are those who say the war on drugs is not worth fighting. Those people are wrong.' He added that this was 'a sentence from which there is no escape and no return'.

HOW MUCH DID EMMA KNOW?

Flanked by her lawyers and enforcement officers, meanwhile, Emma Coronel was whisked out of the courtroom and into a waiting SUV. Less than half the age of her husband, the 29-year-old ex-beauty queen had been branded in the US media as a 'narco Barbie'; fiercely loyal to her husband, she refused to talk to the waiting press.

Coronel has always sought to portray herself as a loving wife and doting mother, insisting she had no involvement in or knowledge of the brutal world of the Sinaloa cartel. 'I don't know my husband as the person they are trying to show him as,' she told the *New York Times* toward the end of the trial, 'but rather I admire him as the human being that I met, and the one that I married.'

In the meantime, other accounts have emerged that paint quite a different picture of her. Did she, as some believe, play an active role in Guzmán's second – and most spectacular – prison escape? At the trial, former Sinaloa cartel lieutenant Dámasco López Nuñez testified that she attended key meetings and approved the purchase of land alongside the jail as well as a GPS-equipped armoured truck that was able to pinpoint the precise position of her husband's cell.

Innumerable incriminating texts between Guzmán and Coronel were also read out in court – instructions to hide away weapons or jokes about buying an AK47 for their seven-year-old daughter – all of which suggested she was well acquainted not only with El Chapo's criminal life but also the inner workings of the Sinaloa cartel.

Her own family could also hardly be described as being of unblemished character. Both her father and brother had connections with the Sinaloa cartel; they were arrested on the Mexican border in 2013 and given lengthy prison sentences for smuggling firearms and drug trafficking.

Of course, the notion of an ageing, wealthy and powerful gangster with the young model wife is the stuff of cliché. Coronel, who grew up in rural poverty, was just 17 when she came to the notice of El Chapo Guzmán – then almost three times her age. It could surely be argued that, in her position, Coronel has no other option but to play the devoted wife and mother.

Even if she wanted to, she was simply too deeply involved, as the wife of the most powerful drugs baron of the modern age, to be allowed to walk away scot-free. In spite of this, it's clear that in Guzmán's eyes, however, she is more than a mere trophy wife – indeed, it would seem he trusts her implicitly.

Since her husband's incarceration, there has been plenty of speculation as to whether Emma Coronel Aispuro could herself be indicted. One anonymous source within the federal law enforcement agency was quoted by the *New York Post* as saying: 'She's being investigated for conspiracy in this country.'

Thus far, however, the United States government seems to have shown little interest in pursuing this path any further. Perhaps now that they have their man, she is simply no longer of any great interest to the Drugs Enforcement Agency.

A JUROR SPEAKS OUT

Throughout the El Chapo trial, cameras had been strictly forbidden in the courtroom and the jurors, unsurprisingly, were ordered by Judge Cogan to remain anonymous. Following the guilty verdict on 12 February, they were now legally free to speak to the press, even if Cogan still strongly advised against it for their own safety and that of their families.

One jury member broke ranks, however, and gave a two-hour interview to online current affairs channel *VICE News*. Requesting anonymity and insisting that even their gender be withheld from the public 'for obvious reasons', the juror revealed that throughout the trial they had routinely ignored the judge's instructions not to discuss the case among themselves, explaining that they had also regularly checked journalist's Twitter feeds and followed the story in the media.

The juror told interviewer Keegan Hamilton that an early concern of the jury was that Guzmán was being held in solitary confinement and they wondered if 'he was going to be in solitary confinement for the rest of his life, because if he was, they wouldn't feel comfortable finding him guilty'.

The juror claimed that several of their colleagues had clearly made their minds up before even hearing a word of evidence, and that two of the jurors had effectively refused to participate in the process, one saying, 'I'm here, I don't care what you decide, guilty or not guilty.'

Even though they disputed the credibility of some of the prosecution witnesses, the jury nevertheless agreed that the evidence against Guzmán in the form of videos, intercepted texts and wiretapped conversations was overwhelming. The juror concluded that Guzmán was guilty beyond any doubt, but that he was also undoubtedly a product of a difficult background that few Americans would be able to comprehend: 'He was just living a life that he only knew how to live since he was young, so it was something normal to him, and not normal to the rest of us.'

The *VICE* story was published on 20 February 2019, and Guzmán's defence team was quick to react. One of his attorneys, Eduardo Balarezo, called the report: 'Deeply concerning and distressing.' If the juror's allegations were true, he went on to say, it was clear that 'Joaquín did not get a fair trial... The information apparently accessed by the jury is highly prejudicial, uncorroborated and inadmissible – all reasons why the Court repeatedly warned the jury against using social media and the internet to investigate the case.'

The implications were clear: their phones had been confiscated during the day, but if the jurors were reading about the case in the media when they returned home each evening, then Guzmán's defence team could legitimately seek a new trial.

In April, however, federal prosecutors from the Eastern District of New York filed a lengthy report declaring that the *VICE* story had merely contained 'unsworn hearsay and double-hearsay allegations' that were 'contradicted by the trial record in material respects'. Defence attorney Jeffrey Lichtman was hardly surprised by the ruling: 'We've said from the start that the Joaquín Guzmán trial was more of an inquisition, a show trial, than an exercise in true American justice.'

Following the verdict, Guzmán was immediately returned to his confinement cell at the Metropolitan Correctional Center, a fortress-like jail in lower Manhattan. After an earlier postponement, Guzmán was informed that full details of his punishment would be delivered on 17 July 2019.

THE FATE OF EL CHAPO

On the morning of the sentencing, Guzmán was delivered to the eighth-floor courtroom of the Federal District Court in Brooklyn at half past nine. Looking dishevelled, in poor health, wearing a loose-fitting grey suit and sporting a newly grown moustache, the world's most notorious narco don awaited his fate.

As Judge Brian Cogan quickly made clear, the crimes for which Guzmán had been found guilty had a punishment mandated in federal law. He admitted, however, that even if there had been any possible leeway in the decision, he was absolutely certain that the 'overwhelming evil' of El Chapo's actions called for the harshest possible sentencing. He pronounced the verdict that Joaquín Guzmán Loera should serve a life sentence plus a consecutive 30 years, and he also ordered him to pay back a staggering $12.6 billion (£10bn) in forfeiture.

Judge Cogan permitted Guzmán to address the court. 'You have the right to be heard. Is there anything you would like to say?' Remaining seated, and through a Spanish interpreter, Guzmán gave thanks to his family and defence attorneys and 'all the people who prayed for me, their prayers have given me the strength to bear this torture that I have been under for the last 30 months'.

He then launched an attack on the United States' authorities and the manner in which he had been held captive. 'The conditions of my confinements under which I've lived for the last 30 months have been total torture. I have been forced to drink unsanitary water. I have been denied access to fresh air and to sunlight. The only light that I get in my cell comes through a duct, and the air that comes into the cell is forced in and it makes my ears, my throat, my head hurt. In order to sleep, I have to use plugs made out of toilet paper in my ears because of the noise that the air duct makes and this has affected me during this time.

'When I was extradited to the United States I expected to have a fair trial, a trial where justice would be blind and where my fame, my reputation, would not be a determining factor in the administration of justice. But what happened was actually the opposite even though you, Your Honor, gave the jury instructions to not watch media – and the jury promised to follow the rules. They did the opposite. They looked at all the articles where I was exposed to the most horrible accusations against me, which were not true. These accusations damaged my opportunity to be judged only on the evidence presented at trial.

'Since the Government of the United States is going to send me to a prison where my name will not ever be heard again, I take advantage of this opportunity to say there was no justice here. My case was stained and you denied me a fair trial when the whole world was watching and where the press was present, judging everybody's actions at every moment. And this then can be denied to any other person in other cases where nobody's watching. What happened here leaves very clear that the United States is not better than any other corrupt country of those that you do not respect. Thank you, Your Honor.'

Following Guzmán's statement, assistant US attorney Gina Parlovecchio delivered a short but damning rebuttal. 'This defendant is uniquely deserving of a life sentence… as the jury found, the defendant was one of the principal leaders of one of the world's most violent and prolific drug cartels… [he] reached this benchmark because of his unmitigated use of violence and corruption. Overwhelming evidence during the trial showed this defendant's vicious use of violence against dozens of murder conspiracy victims.

'But there are millions of other victims impacted by the devastation and death of the defendant's drugs that he and his associates pumped onto the streets and communities throughout this country, drugs for which the defendant reaped billions of dollars in blood money.

'Throughout his criminal career, this defendant has not shown one shred of remorse for his crimes and you heard that today. He is not sorry for his crimes. He speaks of lack of respect for human dignity. He had no respect for the human dignity of his murder conspiracy victims or the millions of people he poisoned with his drugs.

'Instead of taking responsibility, throughout his 25-year reign as a leader of the Sinaloa cartel, this defendant constantly obstructed justice and endangered the lives of law enforcement and other innocent people in the process. A life sentence plus 30 years will protect the public from this defendant who has shown that he will not be deterred from committing horrific crimes. A sentence of life plus 30 years is a just sentence for this defendant.'

NO ESCAPE

Given his past record for audacious jailbreaks, it was inevitable that Guzmán would find himself holed up in one of America's highest-security prisons. Two days after sentencing, he was taken by helicopter to the Administrative Maximum US Penitentiary in Florence, Colorado. Known informally as ADX Florence, this type of 'supermax' prison provides a higher level of custody even than a maximum-security facility.

Nicknamed the 'Alcatraz of the Rockies', ADX Florence houses prisoners deemed too dangerous or too great a security risk to be contained in other correctional facilities. Among the other captives at ADX Florence were some of America's most notorious criminals: Ramzi Yousef, serving life plus 240 years for his role in the 1993 World Trade Center bombing; Richard Reid, the 'Shoe Bomber', who attempted to detonate an explosive on a transatlantic flight; Theodore Kaczynski, the Harvard-educated 'Unabomber', serving eight life sentences; Terry Nichols, one of the Oklahoma City bombers, serving 161 consecutive life sentences. Few of the 400 or so inmates at ADX Florence could expect to be freed.

Prisoners are confined in a 7 × 12 feet (2.1 × 3.6 m) reinforced concrete cell for 23 hours each day; they are handcuffed and shackled when removed from their cells. Guzmán's attorney Jeffrey Lichtman remarked that conditions at ADX Florence amounted to 'more torture… it's just awful'. Even the jail's warden from 2003 to 2005, Robert Hood, had harsh words to say about the establishment. 'This is not built for humanity. I think that being there, day by day, it's worse than death.'

Within the prison is an ultra-secure unit known as 'Range-13', where prisoners have almost no human contact, being confined under camera surveillance 24 hours a day and being allowed only one 15-minute, non-legal phone call per month: barring the unlikely event of a successful appeal or a dramatic change in circumstances, this will be Guzmán's home for the rest of his life.

In spite of his fabulous wealth and the protection of a small army of followers back in his home country, the conviction of Joaquín Archivaldo Guzmán Loera ultimately demonstrated that – as far as the US justice system was concerned, at least – no man is truly above the rule of the law. For almost three decades, the most infamous modern-day narco lord had been able to go about his business in the most brutal ways imaginable, largely unhindered by the Mexican authorities – many of whom were in his direct employ.

Yet although El Chapo was now out of the picture, the Sinaloa cartel – the organization that had been run with such ruthless effectiveness – was far from terminally damaged.

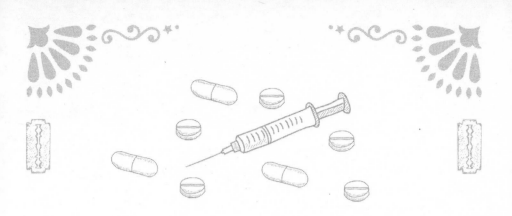

CHAPTER 9:
BUSINESS AS USUAL

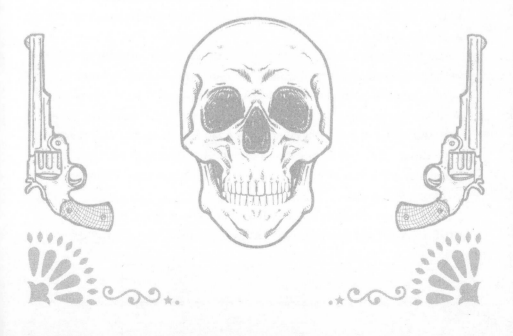

El Chapo himself may have been removed from the field of play, but in the world of the Mexican drug cartels, life and commerce were to carry on regardless. With Guzmán incarcerated in a Manhattan jail for more than two years before his trial, an inevitable bloody power struggle had already played out, often on the streets of Sinaloa. The power vacuum left by Guzmán's extradition resulted in an escalation of violence not seen since the height of drug wars almost a decade earlier. Indeed, by Easter 2017 there had already been 500 drug-related murders in Sinaloa alone.

And the manner of execution was as brutal and gruesome as ever: decapitations, dismembered bodies dumped on roadsides, kidnappings, death threats to police officers and family members.

Adrián López, editor of the Sinaloa newspaper *Noroeste*, remarked on how the cartel operated. 'Something the Sinaloa cartel did well was to have these cells in which everyone made good money, but they also got along… There was a Mafia model in which the main interest was everyone doing well.'

But this system worked only when there was a figure like El Chapo Guzmán, with the overarching authority to deal unequivocally with disputes. The lack of a 'patriarchal' leader led to a very clear generational split with the younger leaders often more concerned with showing off their wealth than following long-established codes of behaviour.

According to Mike Vigil, former chief of international operations for the US Drug Enforcement Agency: 'They just don't have the street smarts and they don't understand that the Sinaloa cartel functions like a global corporation,' he remarked, explicitly citing El Chapo's sons. 'The only thing they know is violence. They want the people to fear them, but [heading a cartel] is much more than that.'

Before he was extradited to the United States, Guzmán had reached an agreement with his former partner, Ismael El Mayo Zambada, and his sons, Ovidio, Guzmán López, Iván Archivaldo Salazar and Alfredo Guzmán Salazar, as to the way the Sinaloa would operate in his absence. However, the two parties had fundamentally different views on the way the cartel should be run.

BULLET IN THE HEAD

Award-winning Mexican journalist Javier Valdez, a specialist in the world of the drug cartels, reported in February 2017: 'The only person with any influence and power within the organization is Ismael Zambada, but he has not shown the same level of violence as [Guzmán's] sons or his brother Aureliano Guzmán and this has led to misunderstandings between them… They don't want to take his advice. They are much more violent and are more sympathetic toward weapons than toward words, and that is very dangerous.'

Valdez, a fearless investigator, had previously remarked that his work was 'like being on a blacklist… The government's promises of protection are next to worthless if the cartels decide they want you dead… Even though you may have bullet-proofing and bodyguards, [the cartels] will decide what day they are going to kill you.'

His words proved to be sadly prophetic: three months later, on 15 May 2017, a block away from the offices of *Ríoduce*, the newspaper he had founded, Valdez was dragged from his car and shot through the head. Even before the drug wars, Mexico had been one of the most dangerous countries in the world to be a journalist, and it still has some of the highest levels of unsolved crimes against the press. More than 300 Mexican journalists or members of the media have either been murdered or have disappeared since 2007.

MYSTERY MAN

Nobody is certain as to the exact number of El Chapo Guzmán's off-spring – so much of his background story is still unknown or open to speculation. The 'official' count is 15, but by some estimates he has fathered 24 children. By no means all of Guzmán's children are involved in drug crime, although four of them – Ovidio Guzmán López, Iván Archivaldo Guzmán, Jesus Alfredo Guzmán Salazar and Joaquín Guzmán López – are significant figures in the Sinaloa cartel. These are widely referred to in the Mexican media as 'Los Chapitos' or 'Los Minores' (The Minors).

Another key name in the internal power struggle with Los Chapitos was Dámaso López, a senior Sinaloa leader and long-standing associate of El Chapo. Nicknamed 'El Licenciado' (The Graduate) because he had studied law at university, López was believed not only to have played a fundamental role in organizing Guzmán's first prison escape in 2001, but he also used his position and family contacts (his father had been a regional attorney general) to bribe officials on behalf of the Sinaloa. At the time of his second capture, in February 2014, Guzmán himself is said to have regarded López as his natural successor, a role López evidently saw for himself following Guzmán's extradition. That's why he entered into an alliance with the Sinaloa's 'upstart' rivals, the Jalisco New Generation cartel.

According to a letter reportedly hand-written by Jesús Alfredo and Iván Alrchivaldo Guzmán, López had invited them and Ismael Zambada to an important conference meeting held on 4 February 2017, in Badiraguato in the heart of Sinaloa territory. According to Mike Vigil, 'When they showed up, they ran into a barrage of bullets from at least five or six individuals; they killed some of their bodyguards, but they were able to get away.' A successful coup would have enabled López to seize leadership of the Sinaloa; instead it sowed the seeds of his own downfall.

In January 2013, the US Treasury had identified López as one of the Sinaloa's principal figures and positioned his photograph one rung below El Chapo on a widely circulated hierarchy chart, labelled 'newly designated top lieutenant'. He was sanctioned for his 'significant role in international narcotics trafficking'. Two months later, López was indicted on charges of drug-trafficking and money laundering, alleging that the proceeds of his criminal activities amounted to some $280 million (£222m).

The incident at Badiraguato was thought to have alerted the authorities, keen to avoid a bloodbath in the wake of El Chapo's incarceration. It was also believed by some that although he might have felt himself in a relatively safe position as a member of a politically well-connected family, he was 'handed over' for siding against the Guzmán family who, after all, still held considerable 'influence' in some official circles. Los Chapitos also regarded López as being behind the ransacking of their grandmother's home in the mountain town of La Tuna in June 2016.

On 2 May 2017, troops and members of the Federal Ministerial Police in masks and full battle gear burst into an apartment block in Colonia Verónica Anzures, an upmarket residential neighbourhood of Mexico City, where they arrested Dámasco López, bringing to an end any ambitions he might have had of becoming the next El Chapo.

Mexico's president Andrés Manuel López Obrador lauded the arrest as a major breakthrough in the war against the drug cartels – 'the detention of another key objective in the battle against criminality'. Immediately following news of the arrest, the United States government filed a request for his extradition. The Mexican government approved the request the following January.

On 6 July 2018, officials handed him over at the border between

Ciudad Juárez, Mexico and El Paso, Texas where he was held awaiting trial. On 30 November 2018, 52-year-old López was given a life sentence at the federal court Alexandria, Virginia. He also agreed to co-operate with officials investigating the murder of Javier Valdez – in which he was suspected of being involved. And, of course, the following year he would also give evidence at the trial of El Chapo.

LIFE AFTER THE KINGPINS

When Guzmán was placed safely behind bars in July 2019, both the American and Mexican authorities were keen to declare publicly how great the impact his conviction would have on the cross-border drugs trade. This was hardly surprising since El Chapo's trial alone is estimated to have cost the United States more than $50 million (£40m).

But experts outside the agencies were telling a more nuanced story. 'The conviction of Chapo Guzmán was a great moral victory because it subjected him to the rule of law,' former DEA chief Mike Vigil told NBC News. 'The conviction, though, has done nothing to impact the Sinaloa cartel because it remains the most powerful cartel in Mexico.'

Furthermore, the Mexican government's strategy of going after these 'kingpins' was brought into question, since it seemed inevitably to result in an explosion of violence, splinter groups within cartels fighting bloody battles over control of territories.

According to Guadalupe Correa-Cabrera, a professor of policy and government at the George Mason University, 'We have had so many narcos dead or arrested and extradited to the United States, and what are the implications of that? None,' she declared. 'It's irrelevant because we have seen this so many times repeating itself.'

El Chapo was effectively neutered by his extradition to the United States in January 2017. By the time of his incarceration more than two years later, with Dámaso López also removed from the scene, the Sinaloa had passed through its most brutal period of bloodletting. 'El Mayo', Ismael Zambada, had stayed largely in the background throughout the dispute between López and Los Chapitos, and as the remaining leader of the cartel's 'old guard' has maintained his overall control.

The elusive Zambada has long been one of the stars of the United States Drug Enforcement Agency's 'most wanted' list. Former DEA chief Mike Vigil made it clear that the main reason he remained out of the reach of the authorities was his refusal to leave his home in the mountain region between Sinaloa and Durango. A helicopter attack by the Mexican authorities, he claimed, 'would be heard for miles' and the rings of security at ground level surrounding Zambada would make his capture 'incredibly difficult'.

Vigil contrasted Zambada's attitude with that of his predecessor. 'The reason Chapo Guzmán was captured is because he has an obsession with women and he decided to come down from the mountains and into the mouth of the *lobo* [wolf].' By moving into the city, El Chapo lost his best natural advantage against the authorities.

'THE MOUSE' IS TRAPPED

With Zambada effectively out of bounds, the Mexican government turned its attention toward Los Chapitos. On 17 October 2019, an intense gun fight broke out in the city of Culiacán, the state capital of Sinaloa. Mexico's security minister, Alfonso Durazo, reported that a patrol of more than 30 National Guard military police came under attack from within a house in the city. They returned fire and when they entered the building, they discovered and arrested Ovidio Guzmán López, El Chapo's son known as 'El Ratón' (The Mouse).

The 29-year-old had been part of his father's gang since his teenage years, and although regarded as a significant member of the Sinaloa cartel he was younger and less influential than his brothers. According to El Chapo's lawyer, Jeffrey Lichtman, the arrest had been sparked by a warrant for Ovidio's extradition issued in February 2019 by a federal judge in Washington DC; he was charged with trafficking cocaine, methamphetamine and marijuana.

Following the arrest, Durazo reported that the security forces found themselves surrounded by a 'a greater force' of cartel gunmen, and that within hours they had withdrawn from the house, leaving Ovidio Guzmán a free man.

Open warfare briefly broke out in the city as cartel forces, donning their characteristic black ski masks, swarmed through Culiacán in a running battle with police and soldiers. The gunmen attacked apartment blocks occupied by the families of military personnel, taking more than a dozen hostages. As fighting raged across the city for around four hours, a police station was burned to the ground, 13 lives were lost and hundreds of people were injured. Social media were swamped with cellphone videos of the fierce gun battles, screaming residents fleeing in panic and black smoke clouds rising from burning vehicles.

The Mexican authorities initially claimed that Ovidio had been discovered during a routine search, but defence secretary Luis Cresencio Sandoval later admitted it was a planned operation, yet few answers were given as to how it could have gone so badly wrong.

Police sources claimed that it had been carried out by 'rogue security forces without proper authorization', but the events made headline news across the world, forcing Mexico's heavily criticized president, Andrés Manuel López Obrador, to defend the actions of his forces.

Claiming that the withdrawal was intended to save the lives of innocent civilians, the government released an extraordinary video of the event. 'We want everything to be known. That's how we demonstrate the responsibility of the actions taken in a complex, difficult and very serious situation,' the president said. 'It's how we demonstrate that the most important thing is to protect citizens, to protect life.'

Filmed as Sinaloa forces began their siege of the house where Ovidio was being held against a background of intense gunfire, a Mexican soldier is seen forcing his captive to make a phone call to his brothers demanding that they abandon their rescue attempt. 'Tell your people to stop this!' he can be heard saying. Although Ovidio can be heard complying, it seems instead to have turned into a flashpoint for the cartel's terrifying show of strength; they had nothing less than a military-grade arsenal, including armoured vehicles, machine guns, and rocket-launchers capable of bringing down a helicopter.

As defence secretary Sandoval argued, his men were outnumbered and would have had to use even more powerful firepower to defeat the cartel force, and that 'would have inevitably put civilians at risk'.

In the face of fierce criticism, President Obrador remained unrepentant. 'Decisions were made that I support, that I endorse, because the situation turned very bad and lots of citizens were at risk... You cannot value the life of a delinquent more than the lives of the people.' The debacle would nevertheless prove to be a grave humiliation for the Mexican government and was regarded by many of Obrador's opponents as setting a dangerous precedent.

It was also another sign of the enduring strength of the Sinaloa cartel. At the end of January 2020, with El Chapo locked away and an uneasy truce in place with its biggest rivals, Jalisco New Generation cartel, the United States Drugs Enforcement Agency reaffirmed their belief that the Sinaloa was still the biggest cartel that 'maintains the most expansive footprint in the United States'. It was, they stated, 'the greatest criminal drug threat to the United States' and that there were no other organizations 'positioned to challenge them'.

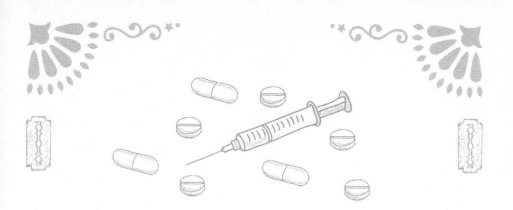

CHAPTER 10:
THE NEW THREAT

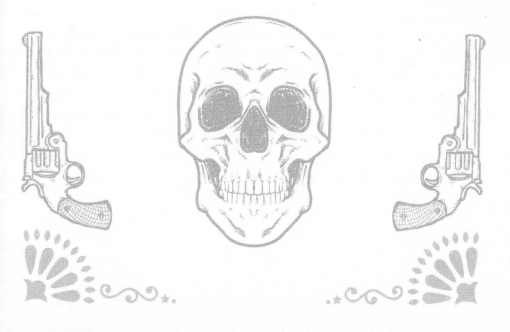

Like any other successful business corporation, one of the reasons the Mexican cartels have been able to survive and prosper is that, time and time again, they have shown themselves to be adaptable. If manufacturing costs or fashions in drug use change, production is altered accordingly. Recent years have seen the cartels diversifying their interests as the profit margins from the production and trafficking of synthetic opioids eclipses those of traditional fare, such as cocaine and heroin. The most potent of these is fentanyl.

First approved for medical use in the United States in 1968, fentanyl was created in 1960 by Belgian physician Paul Janssen as a powerful treatment to help cancer patients cope with the intense pain that followed surgery. It is around 100 times stronger than morphine – and in some of its 'structural analogues' such as carfentanil, which is used in tranquilizer darts on large animals like elephants, around 10,000 times stronger.

During the 1990s, opioids were heavily prescribed for routine pain management, especially in the United States. As was the case with morphine in the 19th century, these medications turned out to be considerably more addictive than many health professionals had at first imagined.

By the start of the 21st century, the US authorities acknowledged that the country was in the grip of a fully fledged opioid crisis. Black-market fentanyl first began to make its mark after 2007, when physicians were instructed to cut back on prescriptions for the opioid OxyContin after the government sued its manufacturer for misleading the public about the risks of addiction. Many of those with addictions turned to heroin, and dealers began mixing it with fentanyl for a faster effect.

Prescription fentanyl usually takes the form of a 'lollipop', or patch, that slowly releases the dosage through the skin, and is usually administered for a few days after major surgery before the patient is weaned off it on to less powerful painkillers. Its illegal counterpart is produced in pill form and sold on the street as Apache, China Girl, Goodfella and Murder 8 among many other colourful names.

SPIKE IN DEATHS

United States government figures show that heroin and cocaine had been responsible for most of the deaths caused by drug overdose before 1999; over the following 15 years, deaths attributable to either prescription or illicit opioids gradually came to dominate that list.

The year 2017, however, saw a startling spike of 70,237 drug-related deaths, of which almost 70 per cent were opioid-related – and 28,466 of those were a result of fentanyl. Fentanyl began to make mainstream headline news as celebrated artists such as Prince, Tom Petty, Lil Peep and Mac Miller succumbed to overdoses. It's thought that many of those who died would not even have been aware that they were using fentanyl.

It's evident that the root of America's opioid crisis was caused by a combination of aggressive marketing by 'Big Pharma' and the failure of successive governments to put a stop to these practices while also failing to provide treatment programmes for those affected. But the dramatic acceleration in the use of fentanyl during the 2010s was exacerbated by a familiar source. It should come as no surprise to find that almost all of the illegal fentanyl reaching the United States has been trafficked by the Mexican cartels, who are increasingly behind its production.

In November 2019, Mexico's Public Safety Secretary, Alfonso Durazo, openly indicated that the abortive attempt to arrest El Chapo's son, Ovidio Guzmán López, had been because of his involvement in the trafficking of opioids. 'One of the reasons for America's interest,' he claimed, was the suspected 'tie between this alleged criminal with the importation of fentanyl to the United States'. It further came to light that a month before the operation, America's Drug Enforcement Agency had carried out a covert fact-finding trip to Culiacán and afterwards issued a statement acknowledging the changing face of their work. 'The profit margins for fentanyl and methamphetamine are now driving the drug trade by the cartels.'

Although at one time fentanyl was largely produced in China's Hubei province, the cartels – now mainly the Sinaloa and Jalisco New Generation – quickly used their powerful global links to buy vast quantities for export into the USA. At first, fentanyl was readily available through the international mail system, but a crackdown by the Chinese authorities in May 2019 acted as a stimulus for its illegal production in Mexico.

Global terrorism expert Scott Stewart discussed the process in an interview with PRI's *The World* in June 2019. 'Some of [the fentanyl] is coming in directly from China – that's already made and manufactured – but then we're also seeing the precursor chemicals come into Mexico and then the Mexican cartels are synthesizing fentanyl in their labs. It's actually an easier drug to synthesize than methamphetamine. So, these Mexican superlabs are pretty well positioned, both in terms of their supply chain to China but also because of their ability to synthesize the drug due to their experience in the methamphetamine trade.'

It's both the astronomical profitability and ease of production that appeal to the cartels. Estimates from the DEA in 2019 were that fentanyl cost between $1,400 (£1,120) and $3,000 (£2,410) a kilo to produce

- and would have a street retail value of over $1 million (£800,000). 'It's much more lucrative,' said Stewart. 'So, essentially, smuggling one kilogram of fentanyl is roughly the equivalent of smuggling 50 kilograms of heroin into the US.'

Besides the profits involved, there are also significant logistical advantages. In the first instance, it doesn't have a growing season like opium poppies do. 'You don't need a lot of land to cultivate it, like you do opium poppies,' continued Stewart. 'Basically, you can fabricate or synthesize it any place that you have the chemicals available. It's also compact to smuggle. It's lucrative, easy to make and easy to smuggle. It really is a dream drug for Mexican organized crime.'

The switch toward synthetic opioid, however, is also having a tangible impact on Mexico's rural economy. In 2106, an anonymous drug trafficker working for the Sinaloa cartel told Al Jazeera news: 'Our clients in the US now just ask for fentanyl. They don't want heroin from poppy plants because they say that fentanyl is stronger, more potent. It means they can cut it and earn more when they distribute it in the streets.'

DEADLY DRUG

In fact, there is evidence to suggest that an increasing proportion of the cocaine and heroin reaching the streets of the United States is being cut with fentanyl. For the occasional 'social' cocaine user, this creates the added peril of a considerably more addictive product. For heroin-users, the situation is potentially far worse as some drug seizures have identified what was thought to be heroin as 100 per cent fentanyl, making the likelihood of the addict taking a fatal accidental overdose considerably more likely.

One result of the cartels' involvements in the opioid markets has been a collapse in the price of the harvested poppy gum used in the production of heroin in the Sinaloa region – between 2017 and 2019, the price per kilogram of the gum scraped from the flower fell from $1,059 (£850) to $265 (£212). A 2019 study by NORIA – the Network of Researchers in International Affairs – portrayed an even more dramatic picture. The report found that farmers in the south of Mexico – 'in mountainous and extremely marginalized regions of rural Mexico, whose inhabitants depend for their livelihoods on opium production' – were now earning less than 10 per cent of what they had been making 18 months previously.

'There isn't enough land to grow quantities of corn [and] tomatoes for profit,' one farmer told Al Jazeera. 'If everyone in the community did that, we wouldn't earn enough to buy shoes, clothes and school bags for the children.' But now, as NORIA president and study co-author Romain Le Cour Grandmaison remarked: 'If you go to villages in Guerrero, there's kilos of opium paste rotting because no one comes to buy it.'

Mexican President Lopez Obrador claimed in 2019 that his administration sought to generate 'a different kind of economy' and was already moving to offer poppy farmers aid. 'Many of them are being helped, and will be helped. All of them. Even in the presidential debates, I suggested that where there was poppy farming, we could stimulate the production of corn and pay a better-than-fair price for the corn to compensate for (losing) the poppy,' he said.

The promotion of crop substitution is, on the surface, a positive grass-roots step toward fighting Mexico's all-pervasive drug trade, but in the short term it simply cannot hope to make up for the economic damage suffered by the farmers. It also takes time to cultivate new crops; mango and avocado trees, for instance, can take years to grow before they begin to yield fruit.

Meanwhile, one of the great fears for the future of Mexico is that poverty will simply drive some of these 'innocent' poppy farmers more deeply into the world of crime unless offered further financial assistance from the government. 'Some of them have weapons and are now being offered employment by criminal groups as hitmen or other positions,' said Le Cour Grandmaison. 'So you actually have people moving into more dangerous and violent roles.'

NEW CHALLENGES

The first months of 2020, of course, saw the emergence of a new global menace as the Covid-19 pandemic swept from China across the globe. The spread was dramatic and swift: by the end of April 2020 there were more than three million reported cases of the disease resulting in around a quarter of a million deaths.

The unprecedented lockdown, not only of national borders but of large chunks of the world's population confined to their own homes, created a new set of challenges both for the illegal drug trade and the law-enforcement agencies.

In the first instance, costs escalated fast for the cartels as raw materials, many of which emanated from China and the Far East, quickly began to run short – and those that were available came at a heavily inflated price. In February 2020, the wholesale cost of fentanyl rose overnight from 870,000 pesos ($37,000/£30,000) per kilo to over a million pesos ($43,000/£35,000).

But a further problem comes with the question of how to distribute drugs in a time when large numbers of people are not leaving their homes. Stories quickly emerged of 'dial-a-dealer', door-to-door deliveries being made in major population centres such as New York City and Los Angeles, but during its initial stages at least, the Coronavirus pandemic achieved what neither the Mexican or American governments had ever managed in curtailing the trafficking of drugs across the border.

Yet at a time of global crisis, the cartels took a leaf from the book of an older criminal organization. In Italy, the Mafia was born at a time of widespread rural poverty and its activities included providing for the poor. That would, of course, come at a price. During the depths of Italy's own terrible Covid-19 experience in March 2020, Mafia clans across the country established daily home food deliveries to some of their poorest communities. This is what Italian journalist Roberto Saviano describes as 'investing in consensus... desperate people who today receive [their] help will be grateful or, rather, will have to express their gratitude when everything gets back to normal and the clans need labour for their illicit enterprises'.

Similarly, during April 2020, a video posted on Facebook showed El Chapo Guzmán's daughter, Alejandrina, filling cardboard boxes with basic provisions – toilet paper, rice, sugar, oil, facemasks and sanitizer – for distribution to the homeless and needy of Mexico's second city, Guadalajara. The message on the page read: 'We are working and contributing. A great pleasure to visit your homes and give you these Chapo handouts.'

The video itself clearly showed the packages – described by the narrator as 'El Chapo's Provisions' – bearing neatly stencilled images of her father's face and the web address of her 'El Chapo 701' clothing brand, so named after her father's ranking in the 2009 *Forbes* World Billionaires list. Just so there could be no doubt about who their benefactor was, the

As the Coronavirus pandemic seizes hold of Mexico, a man poses with a box of basic foodstuffs given to him by the charitable foundation of Alejandrina Guzmán, daughter of El Chapo. It is branded with the face of the drug lord.

packages were handed out by company employees, each one bearing a medical-style facemask adorned with El Chapo's brand image.

Similar actions have been reported across Mexico, with members of the Gulf and Jalisco New Generation also reaching out to the poor in their communities. Falko Ernst, an analyst with International Crisis Group, was clear about their aims. 'They're trying to leverage the perceived absence of the state for their own good and to become more deeply entrenched in local communities.'

As journalist Roberto Saviano said of the Mafia's actions in Italy during the Covid-19 pandemic: 'The organizations rely on want – if you are hungry, you are not particular about which oven your bread comes from.'

Mexico's drug cartels know this only too well.

APPENDICES

APPENDIX A:

THE NARCOS OF MEXICO, A–Z

In 2009, Mexico's federal authorities published a list of 37 drug lords who, they claimed, 'jeopardized Mexico's national security'. They were grouped according to their cartels and rewards of up to 30 million pesos ($1.3 million in 2009/£1m) were listed alongside each one. By the end of 2020, 25 had been captured, 8 had been killed, 1 was allegedly dead and 3 remained on the run. Of course, that list by no means covers all of Mexico's most notorious narcos before or since. (They are listed here, according to Spanish naming custom, by paternal family name.)

PABLO ACOSTA VILLARREAL (1937–1987), Juárez cartel. Also known as 'El Zorro de Ojinaga' (The Ojinaga Fox). One of the pioneer, pre-cartel Mexican drug lords who trafficked heroin and marijuana until the final years of his life when he established links with the Colombian cocaine suppliers. Laundered drugs proceeds by creating chains of luxury hotels and restaurants. Killed by Mexican police helicopters in an FBI-assisted cross-border raid. He had mentored Amado Carrillo Fuentes, who took over his leadership role following his death.

'The tensions of living in crisis lead people to look for symbolic figures that can help them face danger.' (José Luis González) A statue of El Chapo Guzmán is on display by a bust of Narco Saint Jesús Malverde at his chapel in Culiacán..

RAFAEL AGUILAR GUAJARDO (1950–1993), Juárez cartel. Former police commander of federal security who bribed high-level government contacts. Assassinated by his second-in-command, Amado Carrillo Fuentes.

EDUARDO ALMANZA MORALES (date of birth unknown, unconfirmed death 2009), Gulf cartel/Los Zetas cartel. Also known as 'El Gori II'. Brother of Ricardo and Raymundo, two other drug lords on Mexico's '37 most wanted' list. 15 million pesos reward ($650,000/£500,000). Former Special Forces soldier, trafficked drugs to Mexico from Belize and Guatemala for the Gulf cartel before joining Los Zetas. Suspected executioner of Mexican generals Mauro Enrique Tello Quiñones and Juan Esparza García. According to some sources, he was killed in a shoot-out with the federal police in 2009, but the Mexican authorities still regard him as a living fugitive.

RICARDO ALMANZA MORALES (date of birth unknown, died 2009), Los Zetas cartel. Also known as 'El Gori I'. 15 million pesos reward. Killed by federal police 2009.

RAYMUNDO ALMANZA MORALES (date of birth unknown), Los Zetas cartel. Also known as 'El Gori III'. 15 million pesos reward. Former infantry soldier, he was captured by federal police in Monterrey, Nuevo Léon in 2009.

BENJAMÍN ARELLANO FÉLIX (born 1952), Tijuana cartel. Also known as 'El Min'. One of the six Arellano Félix brothers who took over the Tijuana trafficking route following the disintegration of the Guadalajara cartel. One of Mexico's most powerful drug lords, at one point controlling a third of the cocaine entering the United States. Arrested in 2002 by the Mexican Army, which had been tracking his eldest daughter. Extradited to the US in 2011, receiving a 254-year sentence a year later for racketeering and laundering money.

EDUARDO ARELLANO FÉLIX (born 1956), Tijuana cartel. Also known as 'El Doctor'. Captured after a gun fight with the Mexican federal police in 2008. Extradited to the US in 2012, but received only a 15-year sentence as the judge considered him to be 'less involved in the unsavoury aspects' of cartel activities.

FRANCISCO JAVIER ARELLANO FÉLIX (born1969), Tijuana cartel. Also known as 'El Tigrillo' (Little Tiger). Although there was a $5 million (£4m) bounty on his head, the DEA received an anonymous tip-off as to his whereabouts and he was captured by US coastguards fishing in international waters. Charged with organized crime and money laundering, he received a life sentence in 2007 which was later reduced to 23½ years for co-operating with the authorities.

RAMÓN ARELLANO FÉLIX (1964–2002), Tijuana cartel. Also known as 'Comandante Mon'. Regarded as the most ruthless of the Arellano Félix brothers, he had been wanted by the police for the murder of 12 family members in Baja for a drug-related debt in 1997 and was listed on the United States 'Most Wanted' fugitive chart. In February 2002, he was stopped by a police officer for a traffic violation. He pulled a gun and shot the officer, who returned fire as he was falling to the ground; Arellano Felix died immediately.

PEDRO AVILÉS PÉREZ (1938–1978). Also known as 'El León de la Sierra' (The Mountain Lion). He was the first major Mexican drug smuggler. The eventual leaders of the Guadalajara cartel would learn their trade working for the Avila organization. Killed in a shoot-out with police after being set up by one of his own men – thought to have been Ernesto Fonseca Carillo.

ALFREDO BELTRÁN LEYVA (born 1971), Beltrán Leyva cartel. Also known as 'El Mochomo' (The Desert Ant). Arrested in 2008 by the Mexican army in Culiacán. Extradited to the US 2014. Sentenced to life in prison 2017 and ordered to forfeit $529 million (£421m) to the US government.

ARTURO BELTRÁN LEYVA (1961–2009), Beltrán Leyva cartel. Also known as 'Jefe de Jefes' (Boss of Bosses), 'El Barbas' (The Beard), 'El Botas Blancas' (White Boots), 'La Muerte' (Death). 30 million pesos reward. Known for his ability to infiltrate the highest levels of government, military and the police forces to acquire advance warning of official anti-drug operations. Escaped during a Mexican navy special forces raid on a Christmas party thrown at his luxury home in Cuernavaca in December 2009. A week later, he was tracked down and killed during a 90-minute gun fight.

CARLOS BELTRÁN LEYVA (born 1969), Beltrán Leyva cartel. Little is known about his life or role within the organization. Arrested for possessing illegal firearms, cocaine and travelling under a false identity. He was imprisoned in 2009.

HÉCTOR BELTRÁN LEYVA (1965–2018), Beltrán Leyva cartel. Also known as 'El Ingeniero' (The Engineer), 'H', 'El General' (The General). 30 million pesos reward. Arrested by the Mexican army in October 2014. Imprisoned at Altiplano maximum-security jail, where he died from a heart attack in 2018.

ANTONIO EZEQUIEL CÁRDENAS GUILLÉN (1962–2010), Gulf cartel. Also known as 'Tony Tormenta' (Tony Storm). 30 million pesos reward. Formed the elite private security force Los Escorpiones (The Scorpions). Shot dead in 2010 during a gun battle with Mexican navy in Matamoros. According to some witnesses, more than 100 were killed.

OSIEL CÁRDENAS GUILLÉN (born 1967), Gulf/Los Zetas cartel. Head of the Gulf who founded Los Zetas with 30 deserters from Mexico's elite special forces corps to act as the cartel's armed wing. At the time of his capture in 2003, during a shoot-out between Gulf gunmen and the Mexican army, he was on the FBI's 'Ten Most Wanted' list. Extradited to the US in 2007 and given a 25-year sentence. After he agreed to collaborate with US intelligence, his sentence was reduced and he was moved from a 'supermax' prison to the high-security USP Lewisburg in Pennsylvania. He is due for release in 2024.

AMADO CARRILLO FUENTES (1956–1997), Juárez cartel. Also known as 'El Senor de Los Cielos' (The Lord of the Skies). Seized control of the Juárez cartel after assassinating his boss Rafael Aguilar Guajardo. Given his nickname because of the fleet of jets he used to traffic drugs. In the mid-1990s, he was the most sought-after of Mexico's narco-lords with an estimated fortune of $25 billion (£20bn). In an attempt to avoid detection, Carillo attempted to alter his appearance using plastic surgery. He died during the procedure; the bodies of the two surgeons who operated on him were later discovered encased in concrete inside a steel drum.

VICENTE CARRILLO FUENTES (born 1962), Juárez cartel. Also known as 'El Viceroy' (The Viceroy), 'El General' (The General). Mex$30 million reward. At the time of his arrest in 2014, he was head of the Juárez cartel and one of Mexico's most-wanted drug lords.

VICENTE CARRILLO LEYVA (born 1976), Juárez cartel. Also known as 'El Ingeniero' (The Engineer). 30 million pesos reward. His father, Juárez cartel leader Amado Carillo Fuentes, had not wanted his son involved in the narcotics industry, and so sent him away to study at universities in Switzerland and Spain. Arrested in 2009 and charged with illegal possession of firearms and money laundering.

IGNACIO CORONEL VILLARREAL (1954–2010), Sinaloa cartel. Uncle of Emma Coronel, El Chapo's wife. Also known as 'El Nacho', 'King of Crystal'. 30 million pesos reward. Shot in the head in Zapopan, Jalisco during a gunfight with the Mexican Army 2010.

JORGE EDUARDO COSTILLA SÁNCHEZ (born 1971), Gulf cartel. Also known as 'El Coss', 'Sombra' (Shadow). 30 million pesos reward. Former police officer mentored by Osiel Cárdenas Guillén. Arrested by Mexican marines in Tampico in 2012. Extradited to US 2015. Pleaded guilty to conspiracy to distribute cocaine and cannabis.

JUAN JOSÉ ESPARRAGOZA MORENO (1949–2014?), Juárez/Sinaloa cartel. Also known as 'El Azul' (The Blue One). 30 million pesos reward. Former police officer and one of the founders of the Guadalajara cartel and then the Juárez cartel before going to join El Chapo Guzmán in the Sinaloa. Never apprehended. Thought to have died of a heart attack in 2014. Death remains unconfirmed.

JOSÉ JUAN ESPARRAGOZA JIMÉNEZ (born 1972), Sinaloa cartel. Son of Juan José Esparragoza Moreno. Arrested 2014.

MIGUEL ÁNGEL FÉLIX GALLARDO (born 1946), Guadalajara cartel. Also known as 'El Padrino' (The Godfather), 'El Jefe de Jefes' (The Boss of Bosses). The first significant Mexican drug lord, the first to make large-scale connections with the Colombian cocaine producers. Arrested in 1989 in connection with the murder of DEA agent Enrique 'Kiki' Camarena four years earlier. Received 37-year prison sentence – conceived and organized the division of the Guadalajara cartel from his prison cell. Remains incarcerated.

ERNESTO FONSECA CARILLO (born 1930), Guadalajara cartel. Also known as 'Don Neto'. Uncle to Amado Carrillo Fuentes. Involved in drug-smuggling in Ecuador from the 1960s, later moving his operation to Mexico. Indicted by the US in 1982 for money laundering. Arrested in 1985 for the murder of DEA agent Camarena. He was sentenced to 40 years in prison. This became house arrest in 2016 because of his advanced age.

JUAN GARCÍA ABREGO (born 1944), Gulf cartel. One of the most significant drug lords of the 1980s, led the Gulf cartel through a vast network of corruption that permeated all levels of the government of President Ernesto Zedillo. Documents uncovered showed that the head of the Federal Judicial Police had received $1 million (£800,000). An article in the newspaper *El Financiero* suggested that Abrego had infiltrated the attorney general's office. He also paid bribes to the United States Immigration and Naturalization Service and was able to bring drugs across the border in their buses, which were never stopped at the border. He also paid members of the Texas National Guard to transport cocaine from the south of Texas into Houston. On the FBI's 'Ten Most Wanted' list of 1995, he was arrested in Monterrey in January 1996 and immediately extradited to the United States. Convicted on 22 counts and given 11 consecutive life terms.

TEODORO GARCÍA SIMENTAL (born 1974), Tijuana cartel/Sinaloa cartel. Also known as 'El Teo', 'El Tres Letras' (The Three Letters), 'El K-1'. 30 million pesos reward. Arrested by Mexican federal police in La Paz, Baja and imprisoned 2010.

SERVANDO GÓMEZ MARTÍNEZ (born 1966), Familia Michoacana/ Knights Templar cartel. Also known as 'El Profe' (The Professor), 'La Tuta' (The Teacher). 30 million pesos reward. Arrested by Mexican security forces in Morelia, Michoacán in 2015. In 2019, he was sentenced to 55 years in prison for the kidnapping of a businessman.

JAIME GONZÁLEZ DURÁN (born 1973), Gulf/Los Zetas cartels. Also known as 'El Hummer'. Former elite soldier with Mexico's Grupo Aeromóvil de Fuerzas Especiales (GAFE). He was trained in counter-insurgency and narcotics. Former leader of Los Zetas. Mexico's attorney general regarded him as one of the most violent and dangerous criminals at large. He was believed to have ordered the execution of *narcocorrido* singer Valentín Elizalde. Arrested in 2008 and sentenced to 35 years in Altiplano prison.

ARTURO GUZMÁN LOERA (date of birth unknown, died 2004), Sinaloa cartel. Also known as 'El Pollo' (The Chicken). Younger brother of El Chapo who became one of his closest advisors and ran the cartel while he was incarcerated. Arrested in 2004 and murdered by the Juárez cartel while in prison.

AURELIANO GUZMÁN LOERA (date of birth unknown), Sinaloa cartel. Also known as 'El Guano'. Said to be running cartel trafficking operation in northern Mexico, Arizona and Texas.

IVÁN ARCHIVALDO GUZMÁN SALAZAR (born 1983), Sinaloa cartel. Also known as 'El Chapito' (Little Chapo). Eldest son of El Chapo. Arrested in 2005 and given a five-year jail sentence for money laundering but released when judge ruled on an apparent lack of evidence. The judge, Jesús Guadalupe Luna, was later suspended. Kidnapped along with his brother Alfredo by the Jalisco New Generation cartel in 2016. High-ranking figure within the Sinaloa.

JESÚS ALFREDO GUZMÁN SALAZAR (born 1983), Sinaloa cartel. Also known as 'Alfredillo'. Son of El Chapo known for his showy lavish lifestyle. Thought to be high-ranking figure within the cartel. The only one of El Chapo's sons to be on the DEA's most wanted list.

JOAQUÍN GUZMÁN LOERA (born 1957), Sinaloa cartel. Also known as 'El Chapo' (Shorty). 30 million pesos reward. (US Government offered a further $4 million/£3.1m.) Imprisoned 1995. Escaped 2001. Recaptured 2014. Escaped 2015. Recaptured 2016. Extradited to US 2017. Sentenced to 'life plus 30 years' at ADX Florence 'supermax' prison 2019.

MIGUEL ÁNGEL GUZMÁN LOERA (born 1968), Sinaloa cartel. Also known as 'El Mudo' (The Mute One). Sentenced to 15 years in prison in 2005 for opening fraudulent bank accounts for the presumed purpose of money laundering. His sentence was reduced following an *amparo* and he was released in 2017.

OVIDIO GUZMÁN LÓPEZ (born 1991), Sinaloa cartel. Also known as 'El Ratón' (The Mouse). Son of El Chapo. Arrested briefly during a raid in Culiacán in 2019 but released immediately when government troops feared a bloodbath. Thought to be high-ranking figure within the cartel.

EDGAR GUZMÁN LOPEZ (1986–2008), Sinaloa cartel. Son of El Chapo and his father's chosen successor. Kept away from the family business until he had finished his schooling. Killed as a retaliatory act during the war between the Sinaloa and Beltrán Levya cartels.

RAÚL HERNÁNDEZ BARRÓN (1977–2014), Los Zetas cartel. Also known as 'Flanders 1'. Responsible for co-ordinating drug trafficking in the Veracruz region. Suspected executioner of the *narcocorrido* singer Valentín Elizalde in 2006 after he had recorded a song called 'A Mis Enemigos' (To My Enemies), which glorified El Chapo Guzmán and disrespected the Gulf and Los Zetas cartels. Arrested in 2008 at his home in Coatzintla and imprisoned without a conviction until 2010. Killed in a gunfight with the Mexican federal police in 2014 in Reynosa.

RAÚL LUCIO HERNÁNDEZ LECHUGA (date of birth unknown), Los Zetas cartel. Also known as 'El Lucky', 'Z-16'. At the time of his arrest in 2011, he was thought to be one of the cartel's most senior figures; authorities also found 133 rifles, five grenade-launchers, 29 grenades and 36 pistols at the scene of the raid.

HÉCTOR HUERTA RÍOS (date of birth unknown, died 2019), Beltrán Levya cartel. Also known as 'La Burra' (The Donkey). 15 million pesos reward. Captured in 2009 by the Mexican military at a luxury-car dealership that he'd used to launder drug money. Reported to have been killed in 2019
.

HERIBERTO LAZCANO LAZCANO (1974–2012), Los Zetas cartel. Also known as 'El Lazca', 'Z-3', 'El Verdugo' (The Executioner). 30 million pesos reward (additional $5 million [£4m] offered by the US government). Brutal and sadistic army deserter who led Los Zetas and made his name torturing and decapitating his victims. His favoured method was known as 'La Paleta' (The Popsicle), in which the prisoner was stripped naked and beaten endlessly with a board. He is believed to have personally murdered hundreds of victims, their bodies often fed to the lions and tigers he kept on his ranch. His death had been rumoured several years before he perished in a gunfight with the Mexican navy in Progresso, Coahuila on 7 October 2012. He is regarded as the most powerful Mexican cartel leader to have been killed in action.

JUAN PABLO LEDEZMA (born 1987), Juárez cartel/La Linea. Also known as 'José Luis Fratello', 'El JL'. 15 million pesos reward. Suspected of having orchestrated the murder of El Chapo's brother Arturo Guzmán Loera in prison in 2004. In 2019, it was revealed in court that El Chapo had put a bounty on his head. Ledezma went to ground and remains a fugitive.

DÁMASO LÓPEZ NUNEZ (born 1966), Sinaloa cartel. Also known as 'El Licenciado' (The Graduate). Former law student who was seen as likely heir to El Chapo in the Sinaloa cartel. Ran the Navolato and Los Cabos plazas. Arrested by the Mexican army in Mexico City in 2017. Extradited to the United States in 2018 and received a life sentence. Was a prosecution witness in the trial of El Chapo.

DIONISIO LOYA PLANCARTE (born 1955), Knights Templar cartel. Also known as 'El Tío' (The Uncle). 30 million pesos reward. Arrested in Morelia, Michoacán in 2014 and imprisoned at Altiplano maximum-security jail.

JUAN RAMÓN MATTA-BALLESTEROS (born 1945). Also known as 'El Negro'. Honduran drug-trafficker credited with linking the Colombia cartels with the Mexican traffickers in the early 1980s. He owned an airline company that was used by the CIA to covertly supply arms to Nicaraguan Contras. Arrested for suspected involvement with the

execution of DEA agent Camarena, but he bribed his way out of prison and fled to Honduras. He was eventually extradited to the United States and remains incarcerated.

FLAVIO MÉNDEZ SANTIAGO (born 1975), Los Zetas cartel. Also known as 'El Amarillo' (The Yellow One). 15 million pesos reward. Sanctioned by the United States Treasury under the Kingpin Act for involvement in drug-trafficking. Captured by federal police in Villa de Detla, Oaxaca in 2011.

JOSÉ DE JESÚS MÉNDEZ VARGAS (born 1974), Familia Michoacana cartel. Also known as 'El Chango' (The Ape). 30 million pesos reward. Arrested by federal police in Aguascalientes in 2011. Extradition to US pending.

NAZARIO MORENO GONZÁLEZ (1970-2014), Familia Michoacana/ Knights Templar cartel. Also known as 'El Chayo' (The Rosary), 'El Más Loco' (The Craziest One). 30 million pesos reward. Killed resisting capture by Mexican navy in Tumbiscatío, Michoacán in 2014.

SIGIFREDO NÁJERA TALAMANTES (date of birth unknown, died 2015), Gulf cartel. Also known as 'El Canicón' (The Marble). 15 million pesos reward. Captured 2009. Died of a heart attack in Altiplano prison 2015.

ÓSCAR ORLANDO NAVA VALENCIA (born 1971), Milenio cartel. Also known as 'El Lobo' (The Wolf). Leader of the Milenio. Operated in Michoacán, Colima, Jalisco, Mexico City, Nuevo León and Tamaulipas, where the cartel produced marijuana and heroin. Arrested by Mexican federal police in 2009. Extradited to United States in 2011. Serving a 25-year prison sentence in Houston, Texas.

JUAN NEPOMUCENO GUERRA CÁRDENAS (1915-2001). Also known as 'Don Juan', 'El Padrino de Metamoros' (The Godfather of Metamoros).

The original Mexican drug lord, began life as a bootlegger smuggling whisky across the border into Texas during the 1930s. In the 1970s, his nephew Juan García Abrego used his uncle's political connections and networks to traffic narcotics, creating what would ultimately become known as the Gulf cartel. In spite of a long life of crime, he was reputed never to have spent more than a few hours in jail. He died of natural causes in 2001.

NEMESIO OSEGUERA CERVANTES (born 1966), Milenio/Jalisco New Generation cartel (CJNG). Also known as 'El Mencho'. Former methamphetamine producer and drug dealer in California. Deported to Mexico in 1992. Joined Milenio cartel and created its armed wing. When the Milenio split, he named his group the CJNG, which soon became one of Mexico's most profitable drug-trafficking organizations in its own right – the Mexican government estimates that it controls assets of at least $50 billion (£40bn). Said to be in hiding in the rural terrains of Jalisco, where he is guarded by a private army. Regarded as the most senior drug lord currently at large. The reward for his capture is 30 million pesos from the Mexican government and $10 million (£8m) from the United States.

HÉCTOR LUIS PALMA SALAZAR (born 1940), Guadalajara/Sinaloa cartel. Also known as 'El Güero' (Blondie). Arrested for drug trafficking in 1978 and served eight years in a US prison. On release, became a hitman for Miguel Ángel Félix Gallardo and worked his way up to become one of the leaders of the Guadalajara. Co-leader of the new Sinaloa cartel, alongside El Chapo Guzmán. Arrested in 1995 after a Lear jet he was in crash-landed. Currently imprisoned at Altiplano prison near Mexico City.

SERGIO PEÑA SOLÍS (born 1973), Gulf/Los Zetas cartel. Also known as 'El Concord', 'El Colosio'. 30 million pesos reward. Assumed control of Los Zetas cartel following arrest of Jaime González Durán. Captured

2006 and charged with drug-trafficking and the killing of a local businessman but escaped from prison. Recaptured 2009 trying to flee a police checkpoint in a stolen truck.

RAMIRO PEREZ MORENO (born 1981), Los Zetas cartel. Also known as 'El Rana' (The Frog). Presumed heir to the Los Zetas leadership – following the arrest of Omar Treviño Morales – until his own arrest in Nuevo Laredo weeks later.

ALBERTO PINEDA VILLA (date of birth unknown, died 2009), Beltrán Leyva cartel. Brother of Marco Antonio Pineda Villa. Also known as 'La Borrado' (The Hazel Eyes). 15 million pesos reward. Found dead near Mexico City along with his brother in 2009. The murders were apparently a vendetta thought to have been ordered by Arturo Beltrán Leyva.

MARCO ANTONIO PINEDA VILLA (date of birth unknown, died 2009), Beltrán Leyva cartel. Also known as 'El MP'. 15 million pesos reward. Found dead near Mexico City along with his brother in 2009.

ENRIQUE PLANCARTE SOLÍS (1970-2014), Familia Michoacana and later one of the leaders of the Knights Templar cartel. Also known as 'La Chiva'. Killed in a gunfight with the Mexican navy in Colón, Querétaro.

RAFAEL CARO QUINTERO (born 1952), Guadalajara cartel. Also known as 'Narco of Narcos'. Arrested in 1985 for the murder of DEA agent Enrique 'Kiki' Camarena five years earlier. Also suspected of ordering the murder of American journalist John Clay Walker, who accidentally walked into one of his private parties. Sentenced to 40 years in prison. Released 9 August 2013 to outrage from the United States; a new arrest warrant ordered five days later. Quintero has not been seen in public since. In 2018, he gave an interview to *Huffington Post* claiming that he had not killed Camarena, was no longer involved in drug-trafficking, and lived a quiet life in his mountain home in Mazatlán.

SERGIO ENRIQUE RUIZ TLAPANCO (born 1972), Los Zetas cartel. Also known as 'El Tlapa', 'Z-44'. 15 million pesos reward. Former soldier and police officer. Arrested and imprisoned 2009.

CARLOS ENRIQUE SÁNCHEZ MARTÍNEZ (date of birth unknown), Jalisco New Generation (CJNG)/Nuevo Plaza cartel. Also known as 'El Cholo'. Formed breakaway cartel after ordering the execution of a CJNG financier; leader El Mencho Oseguera Cervantes retaliated by sending the CJNG hit squad after El Cholo – it was unsuccessful and its leader was killed.

LUIS FERNANDO SÁNCHEZ ARELLANO (born 1977), Tijuana cartel. Also known as 'El Alineador' (The Aligner). 30 million pesos reward. Nephew of Eduardo Arellano Félix. Arrested by Mexican army and federal agents of the PGR at fast-food restaurant in Tijuana 2014. Imprisoned at Altiplano maximum-security jail.

GREGORIO SAUCEDA GAMBOA (born 1965), Los Zetas cartel. Also known as 'El Goyo', 'Metro-2'. 30 million pesos reward. Former investigative police officer. Captured in Matamoros in 2009.

HÉCTOR MANUEL SAUCEDA GAMBOA (date of birth unknown, died 2009), Gulf cartel. Also known as 'El Karis'. Ran the cartel's operation in Reynosa. Los Zetas sent an execution squad to seize his plaza, but by the time they arrived he had been killed in a shoot-out with the police.

MIGUEL ÁNGEL TREVIÑO MORALES (born 1970), Los Zetas cartel. Also known as 'Z-40', 'Cuarenta' (Forty). 30 million pesos reward (additional $5 million offered by the US government). Led squad that successfully fought off advances from the Sinaloa in the lucrative Nuevo Laredo plaza. A merciless killer, and by the time of Heriberto Lazcano Lazcano's death, he had effectively seized control of Los Zetas. With US indictments since 2009, Treviño Morales was apprehended by Mexican marines in 2013 and remains imprisoned in Ciudad Juárez. The New York Federal District Court has sought his extradition.

OMAR TREVIÑO MORALES (born 1974), Los Zetas cartel. Also known as 'Z-42', 'L-42', 'Omar'. 30 million pesos reward (additional $5 million offered by the US government). Elder brother of Miguel Ángel Treviño Morales and presumed to have been his successor. Captured in a joint operation by the Mexican Army and Federal Police in 2015.

EDGAR VALDEZ VILLARREAL (born 1973), Los Negros/Beltrán Leyva cartel. Also known as 'La Barbie' (The Barbie), 'El Güero' (Blondie). 30 million pesos reward. Arrested by federal police in Mexico City 2010. Extradited to US 2015. In court, described himself as 'a legitimate businessman'. Sentenced to 49 years in USP Coleman high-security prison, Florida in 2018.

ÉRICK VALENCIA SALAZAR (born 1977), Milenio/Jalisco New Generation(CJNG)/Nuevo Plaza cartel. Also known as 'El 85'. Former high-ranking figure in the Milenio and CJNG cartels. Arrested in an army raid on Zapopan in 2012. After serving five years in prison, he was released at the end of 2017, after which he co-founded a breakaway group. CJNG and Nuevo Plaza are currently at war for territorial control over Guadalajara and Jalisco.

IVÁN VELÁZQUEZ CABALLERO (born 1970), Los Zetas cartel. Also known as 'El Talibán', 'Z-50'. 30 million pesos reward. Principle finance operator and money launderer for the cartel. Captured by the Mexican navy in San Luis Potosi in September 2012. He was extradited to the US in November 2013. In 2017, he was sentenced to 30 years in prison by a federal judge in Laredo, Texas.

SERGIO VILLARREAL BARRAGÁN (born 1969), Beltrán Leyva cartel. Also known as 'El Grande' (The Big One), 'Comeniños' (The Child Eater), 'King Kong'. 30 million pesos reward. Captured during a raid by Mexican marines in the central state of Puebla 2010. Extradited to US 2012.

ISMAEL ZAMBADA GARCÍA (born 1948), Sinaloa cartel. Also known as 'El Mayo', 'El M-Z', 'El Padrino' (The Godfather). 30 million pesos reward (additional $5 million offered by the US government). Remains at large and is still the leader of the Sinaloa cartel.

ISMAEL ZAMBADA IMPERIAL (born 1984), Sinaloa cartel. Son of El Mayo. Also known as 'El Mayito' (Little Mayo) due to his resemblance to his father. Arrested 2015. Extradited to the US 2019. Trial pending.

JESÚS VICENTE ZAMBADA NIEBLA (born 1975), Sinaloa cartel. Son of El Mayo. Also known as 'El Vicetillo' (Little Vicente). 30 million pesos reward. Arrested in Mexico City 2009. Extradited to US 2010. After plea bargain, and giving evidence against other members of the Sinaloa (including El Chapo), he had his sentence reduced to 10 years and a $4 million (£3.2m) fine in 2019.

SERRAFÍN ZAMBADA ORTIZ (born 1990), Sinaloa cartel. Son of El Mayo. Arrested in Arizona 2013. Sentenced to ten years in prison. Given early release 2018.

APPENDIX B:

THE MEXICAN DRUG CARTELS, A–Z

Besides El Chapo Guzmán's Sinaloa cartel, numerous other powerful criminal organizations have operated in the world of the Mexican drug industry over the past four decades. During that time, the balance of power has shifted continually as cartels fought tooth and nail for territorial advantage, forged and broke alliances, splintered into new groups and, in some cases, disappeared altogether when a key leader was killed or arrested by the authorities. Perhaps the most severe indictment of both America's 'War on Drugs' and the Mexican government's inability to grasp control of the situation is that many of these organizations, including the Sinaloa, have been able to continue their activities right up to the present day – and most of those that had been working for organizations that fell apart or disbanded simply began working for other cartels.

LOS ÁNTRAX (THE ANTHRAX), 2010 TO PRESENT

Enforcers for the Sinaloa cartel and de facto personal security force for El Chapo Guzmán's successor, Ismael 'El Mayo' Zambado. The gang operates in Sinaloa's capital city, Culiacán. Leader Rodrigo Aréchiga Gamboa ('El Chino Ántrax') was one of the first drug barons to embrace social media, posting selfies of his opulent lifestyle on Facebook and

Instagram. This ultimately led to his arrest in Amsterdam at the end of 2013 and subsequent extradition to the United States. In March 2020, he was released and placed under house arrest; in May he was reported missing by his parole officer and is now presumed to have returned to Mexico. In a bizarre twist, Mexican model and social media personality Claudia Ochoa Félix was rumoured to have been one of the group's leaders following El Chino's arrest. She denied the reports, but on 14 September 1919 was found dead at her home. The official cause of death was a drug overdose, but many believed it to have been an assassination due to her links with the Sinaloa and Ántrax.

LA BARREDORA (THE SWEEPER TRUCK), 2010 TO PRESENT

Splinter group from the Beltrán Levya cartel based in Acapulco. Bitter rivals of Cártel Independiente de Acapulco and known to have strong links with the Sinaloa. Their brutal hitmen are known as 'El Comando Del Diablo' (The Devil's Command) and were celebrated in a narco ballad of the same name by Gerardo Ortíz – who was himself arrested in 2016 on charges of '*apología del delito*' (criminal exaltation).

BARRIO AZTECA (LOS AZTECAS), 1986 TO PRESENT

Mexican-American gang formed in the 1980s by prisoners incarcerated in El Paso, Texas and Ciudad Juárez in Mexico – an area that although divided by the national border is regarded by most inhabitants as part of the same urban sprawl. Barrio Azteca formed an alliance with La Línia to fight against the Sinaloa cartel. Barrio Azteca are known to control the sale of drugs on the streets and in the jails of both cities. The group is set up along military lines with clearly defined ranks denoting position and responsibility within the organization's hierarchy. In June 2018, leader Eduardo Ravelo was arrested by the Mexican police. At its peak, Barrio Azteca is thought to have numbered 3,000 in El Paso and 5,000 in Ciudad Juárez.

BELTRÁN LEYVA CARTEL, 2008–2014

Allied to the Sinaloa cartel, the four Beltrán Leyva brothers – Marcos Arturo, Carlos, Alfredo and Héctor – played an important role in securing trade routes in the north-eastern border. The brothers effectively infiltrated Mexico's government, judiciary and police force, giving them advanced warning of official anti-drug operations. In January 2008, Alfredo, 'El Mochomo' (The Desert Ant), was arrested by the Mexican army in Culiacán. Five months later, Edgar Millán Gomez, the police commissioner responsible for the arrest was gunned down at his Mexico City home; it was presumed to be a retribution killing. Believing that El Chapo Guzmán was behind the arrest of their brother, the Beltrán Levyas broke away from the Sinaloa and Arturo ordered the brutal assassination of Guzmán's son, Édgar. They allied themselves with the Sinaloa's rivals, the Juárez cartel, and a violent turf war escalated. In 2010, the Beltrán Levya and Los Zetas cartels joined forces against an alliance of the Sinaloa, Gulf and La Familia cartels in Tamaulipas. Alfredo Beltrán Levya was the first of the brothers to be captured and extradited to the United States. Arturo – by this time one of the country's most wanted drug lords – was gunned down during a raid by the Mexican navy's elite special forces unit. Shortly afterwards, Carlos was arrested by the police when he was pulled over while driving and found to be using a forged licence. The cartel was effectively brought to an end in October 2014 with Héctor's arrest by the Mexican army. He died in prison four years later.

COLIMA CARTEL, 1988–1998

Based in the small tourist state on Mexico's southwestern coast, the Colima cartel – led by the three Contreras brothers, Luis, Adán and Jesús – dealt mainly in methamphetamine. During 1997 and 1998, all three brothers were arrested by the Mexican police and the remnants were subsumed into the Sinaloa cartel. In 2016, the once-peaceful region became Mexico's most violent state as the Sinaloa and CJNG cartels fought for territorial control.

LOS CABALLEROS TEMPLARIOS CARTEL (THE KNIGHTS TEMPLAR), 2011–2017

Formed following the 'first death' of La Familia cartel leader Nazario Moreno González, an eccentric, evangelical Christian who wore white robes and produced a pocket-sized code book listing 53 commandments that all cartel members – his 'knights' – were compelled to obey. Known as 'El Más Loco' (The Craziest One), Moreno González was an almost spiritual figure to some in the Michoacán state; prayer books were dedicated to 'Saint Nazario' and narco ballads were written to honour the cartel ('Their fights are like crusades… They say they were like monks, And today they are guerrillas, They have their temples and their camps'). Not only did Los Caballeros seize most of La Familia's activities, they also took over the region's iron mines and the avocado, lime and cattle industries. By this time one of Mexico's most wanted criminals, Moreno González was gunned down on 9 March 2014 following a joint operation by Mexico's army and navy. Los Caballeros would later feud violently with the Cártel de Jalisco Nueva Generación (CJNG, Jalisco New Generation cartel) as it tried to gain control of Michoacán. In September 2017, new cartel leaders Pablo 'El 500' Toscano Padilla and Ezequiel 'El Cheques' Castañeda were gunned down by remnants of La Familia Michoacana on their way to a meeting with CJNG leaders. With most of the original founders dead, the group was effectively disbanded, the remnants joining up with *La Nueva Familia Michoacana*.

CÁRTEL DE JALISCO NUEVA GENERACIÓN (CJNG, 'JALISCO NEW GENERATION'), 2009 TO PRESENT)

When the Milenio cartel – then a 'branch' of the Sinaloa – disintegrated, a new operation emerged headed by Nemesio Oseguera Cervantes ('El Mencho'), Érick Valencia Salazar ('El 85') and Martín Arzola Ortega ('El 53'). After defeating rival splinter group La Resistencia, CJNG rapidly expanded its operation and within six months was already regarded as one of the most significant cartels in Mexico. The group set itself up as protectors of the local population and was originally conscripted by the Sinaloa in their fight against the Los Zetas cartel. In 2011, CJNG declared war on all of Mexico's cartels. In August 2016, they humiliated the Sinaloa by kidnapping two of El Chapo Guzmán's sons; after negotiations, they were released. Although many of the group's leaders were arrested in the late 2010s, El Mencho Cervantes has evaded the authorities and remains Mexico's most wanted criminal, with a US bounty on his head of $10 million (£8m). Meanwhile, in 2020 the US Drugs Enforcement Agency highlighted the Sinaloa and CJNG as the two most significant threats in the battle against the drugs cartels.

LA FAMILIA MICHOACANA CARTEL, 2006–2011

The cartel is thought to have originated among a group of vigilantes who came together to protect the poor of the Michoacán state, taking on kidnappers and drug dealers from other regions, but who gradually transformed into a powerful criminal gang in its own right. During the 1990s, La Familia acted as a paramilitary group for the Gulf cartel's activities in their region before splintering from it to become an independent drug trafficking operation in 2006. In spite of its notorious violence, the cartel described itself as 'a necessary evil', with a strict spiritual and moral code; its leader Nazario Moreno González published his own 'bible' ('I ask God for strength and he gives me challenges that make me strong; I ask him for wisdom and he gives me problems to resolve'). Cartel members were expected to observe religious and family values, to abstain from using the drugs they sold and to take action against those who exploited women and children. The cartel was also known to give loans to churches, schools and farmers. Once the fastest-growing cartel, it became Mexico's main producer of methamphetamines, running numerous laboratories that could produce around 100 pounds (45 kilos) of meth in 8 hours. According to the DEA, La Familia was strongly opposed to selling drugs to Mexicans. The cartel fought a frequently brutal war against another Gulf offshoot, Los Zetas.

In December 2010, following a two-day shoot-out with Mexican federal police, Nazario Moreno González was reported dead by the authorities; in fact, he survived and led a breakaway cartel, Los Caballeros Templarios (The Knights Templar), taking many key leaders and groups from within La Familia. In 2011, following the American-led Project Delirium, more than 2,000 members of La Familia were arrested in Mexico and the United States, and what remained of the cartel was effectively disbanded. The remnants would transform into La Nueva Familia Michoacana.

GUADALAJARA CARTEL, 1980–1989

Mexico's largest crime organization during the 1980s splintered following the arrest of leader Miguel Ángel Félix Gallardo in 1989, with two of his most powerful lieutenants, Héctor Luis Palma Salazar and El Chapo Guzmán, forming the breakaway Sinaloa cartel. Other high-ranking figures would go on to form the rival Tijuana and Sonora cartels.

GENTE NUEVA (NEW PEOPLE), 2007 TO PRESENT

This was a cell created to fight for the Sinaloa cartel and repel the Juárez cartel in the key smuggling routes between El Paso and Ciudad Juárez in northwest Mexico – the trade line through which about 70 per cent of cocaine is brought into the United States. Taking advantage of infighting within the Juárez, many members were recruited by Gente Nueva. The group played a significant role in the Juárez cartel's defeat and future marginalization.

GUERREROS UNIDOS (UNITED WARRIORS), 2010 TO PRESENT

Based in Mexico City, Guerreros Unidos are one of at least seven splinter groups from the Beltrán Levya cartel. Founded by Mario Casarrubias Salgado, the organization focuses not only on drug trafficking but also on extortion and kidnapping. In 2014, three members of the cartel were arrested over the disappearance of 43 students, one of whom was discovered with his eyes gouged out and the skin flayed from his face. Guerreros Unidos were effective in recruiting corrupt officials into their organizations; in 2013, 44 police officers were arrested for their involvement with the cartel.

GULF CARTEL, EARLY 1930S TO PRESENT

The oldest of Mexico's cartels, it was founded towards the end of the Prohibition era to smuggle bootleg alcohol into the United States. After Prohibition, it switched to gambling, prostitution and later narcotics. During the 1980s, under the leadership of Juan García Ábrego, the Gulf entered into an agreement with the Colombian Cali cartel which was so successful that by the middle of the 1990s it handled one third of all cocaine shipments and was valued at around $10 billion (£8bn). Ábrego was arrested on 14 January 1996 and was extradited to the United States; he is currently serving 11 consecutive life terms at USP Hazelton in Preston County, West Virginia. The resulting violent power struggle saw the ascendance of Osiel Cárdenas Guillén in July 1999, who assumed the leadership after assassinating his co-leader and close friend Salvador Gómez Herrera – earning himself the nickname 'Mata Amigos' (Friend Killer). As violent confrontation with rival gangs escalated, Cárdenas recruited highly trained military personnel that became known as Los Zetas. When Cárdenas was arrested and extradited to the United States in 2007 following a power struggle, the increasingly influential Los Zetas became an independent cartel. The Gulf continues to be a major influence in its home state, Tamaulipas in north-eastern Mexico, as well as maintaining a presence in the US states of Texas and Georgia.

CÁRTEL INDEPENDIENTE DE ACAPULCO (CIDA) ('INDEPENDENT CARTEL OF ACAPULCO'), 2010 TO PRESENT

Based in the Acapulco region on Mexico's Pacific coast, the Independent cartel formed in 2010, splitting from the Beltrán Levya cartel during the power struggle that followed the death of leader Arturo Beltrán Levya. In February 2018, they were publicly accused of the murder of the political video blogger Nana Pelucas.

JUÁREZ CARTEL, 1970S TO PRESENT

One of the oldest – and once among the most powerful – of Mexico's criminal organizations, the cartel is based around Ciudad Juárez in the state of Chihuaha. In 1993, leader Rafael Aguilar Guajardo was murdered by his lieutenant, Amado Carrillo Fuentes ('El Señor de los Cielos' – The Lord of the Skies) who assumed control. The Juárez became hugely powerful during the 1990s. Fuentes, it was said, was more concerned with negotiating than fighting and much of the cartel's success came from bribing corrupt officials, most famously general Jesus Gutierez Rebollo, then Mexico's highest-ranking drugs officer. Under investigation, Carillo underwent facial plastic surgery in 1997 to avoid arrest but died during the operation. After an internal power struggle, Carillo's brother Vicente assumed power. In 2001, an alliance between the Juárez and Sinaloa cartels broke down when El Chapo Guzmán refused to pay for the right to use their smuggling routes. When El Chapo ordered the execution of Vicente's brother, Carillo Fuentes responded in kind, having El Chapo's brother executed in his prison cell. A full-scale turf war briefly erupted. The cartel attracted the interest of the Mexican government in January 2004 following the discovery of the so-called 'Juárez House of Death', the site of numerous drug executions in Ciudad Juárez; President Calderón sent thousands of troops into the city. In 2014, Vicente Carrillo Fuentes was arrested by the Mexican Army in the town of Torreón, Chihuahua and sent to jail in Puente Grande, leaving the cartel a shadow of its former self.

LA LÍNEA (THE LINE), 2007 TO PRESENT

Active in Chihuahua and the border region of Texas, La Línea was an enforcer unit for the Juárez cartel formed by corrupt active-duty policemen to counter the threat of the Sinaloa cartel, who were attempting to take over the drug-running routes in the region. The group has been linked to frequent notorious violent episodes in Ciudad Juárez, including the Villas de Salvárcar massacre, in which 16 teenagers were murdered at a party on 31 January 2010, and the Chihuahua rehab centre shooting in which 19 were executed.

LA MANO CON OJOS (THE HAND WITH EYES), 2010 TO PRESENT

One of many splinter groups from the Beltran Levya cartel, La Mano Con Ojos centre their activities on the fringes of Mexico City. In 2011, this small group made headlines when, following the arrest of their leader, Óscar Osvaldo García Montoya, two severed heads were left outside Mexican army headquarters with a message from the group claiming responsibility. Following his arrest, Montoya gave a widely publicized interview in which he claimed to have killed more than 300 people during his criminal career. 'I was trained to kill and to sustain myself in life,' he calmly proclaimed to the camera.

MILENIO CARTEL/CÁRTEL DE LOS VALENCIA (VALENCIA CARTEL), 1999 TO PRESENT

Formed by the Valencia family in Michoacán, the Milenio began as cannabis and poppy farmers, selling their produce to larger cartels, and later became heroin-producers. In 2003, following a number of significant arrests, the cartel formed an association with El Chapo Guzmán's Sinaloa cartel, becoming part of what was to be known as the Sinaloa Federation. When leader Óscar Nava Valencia was captured by the police in 2009, the Milenio broke into regional factions, most notably Jalisco New Generation (CJNG) and La Resistencia (The Resistance) who fought a violent battle for territorial control. In 2012, the remnants of the Milenio relocated to Guadalajara. Most of the Valencia family are allied to the CJNG because leader Nemesio Oseguera Cervantes ('El Mencho') is married to a Valencia.

LOS NEGROS (THE BLACK ONES), 2003–2010

An armed security force formed by the Sinaloa to counter the threat of Los Zetas, their equivalent within the Gulf cartel. When the Beltrán Levyas split from the Sinaloa, they took Los Negros with them. Following the death of Arturo Beltrán Levya in 2009, Los Negros followed his second-in-command Édgar Valdez Villarreal; after his arrest in August 2010, the group collapsed.

OAXACA CARTEL, 1980–2011

Trafficking cocaine and marijuana for decades in the southern states of Mexico, the Oaxaca joined forces with the Tijuana cartel in 2003. Founder Pedro Díaz Parada was originally imprisoned for 33 years in 1985; after two long periods on the run, he was finally incarcerated in 2007, leadership being assumed by his brothers Eugenio ('Don Chuy') and Domingo ('Don Cheto').

LA RESISTENCIA (THE RESISTANCE), 2010 TO PRESENT

A splinter group of the Milenio cartel, La Resistencia largely comprised highly trained gunmen from the Sinaloa, Gulf and Knights Templar cartels brought together to expel Los Zetas from Michoacán and Jalisco. For two years, they fought a violent territorial war with the Jalisco New Generation cartel, but they were dealt a heavy blow when founder and leader Ramiro Pozos Gonzalez, alias 'El Molca', was arrested by Mexican police. He was blamed for the massacre of 26 in Guadalajara in November 2016.

SONORA CARTEL, 1989 TO THE 1990S

Created by Miguel Ángel Caro Quintero during the disintegration of the Guadalajara cartel, the Sonora's main activity was the cultivation and trafficking of marijuana. Once disbanded, the remnants joined the Sinaloa and Tijuana cartels.

CÁRTEL DEL PACÍFICO SUR (SOUTH PACIFIC CARTEL), 2010 TO PRESENT

Based in the state of Morelos, this is the group formed from the remnants of the Beltrán Levya cartel. Known for their extreme violence, they notoriously forced children as young as 12 to act as executioners. They became less significant following the arrest of their leaders, Julio de Jésus Radilla Hernández and Víctor Valdéz, in 2011.

TIJUANA CARTEL, 1989 TO PRESENT

Founded by the Arellano-Felix brothers, Benjamín and Ramón, the Tijuana cartel formed when their uncle, Miguel Ángel Félix Gallardo, the leader of the powerful Gudalajara cartel, was incarcerated in 1989. During the 1990s, it was perhaps the most significant organized crime group in Mexico, and controlled trafficking across the strategically important border towns between Mexico and the United States. The group's activities were curtailed by infighting and the government's Operation Tijuana in 2009. Many working for the cartel shifted allegiance to the Sinaloa at this time.

LOS ZETAS CARTEL, 1999 TO PRESENT

Formed as a private army for the Gulf cartel by retired Mexican army lieutenant Arturo Guzmán Decena in 1999, they took their name from Decena's police radio code (Z1). Decena lured 30 army deserters from Mexico's elite GAFE and GANFE forces, many of whom had been trained in commando and urban warfare by the Israeli and US Special Forces. Los Zetas quickly became an essential part of the Gulf cartel's activities, and became especially well known for their brutally violent efficiency and targeting of civilians. The group became even more powerful following the extradition of Gulf leader Osiel Cárdenas Guillén, so much so that they outnumbered the Gulf in numbers and revenue. The new leaders of the Gulf tried to curtail their power, instigating a brief civil war that led to Los Zetas becoming an independent cartel in 2010 under the leadership of Heriberto Lazcano. Thus began a bloody war for control of northeast Mexico's drug routes, drawing in other cartels who wanted strategic alliances. Although internal splits diminished their influence, they remain active in the Mexican drug trade and other criminal activities such as human trafficking and oil pipeline theft.

APPENDIX C:

A BRIEF HISTORY OF NARCOTICS

The scale of the global trade in illegal narcotics, not to mention the mind-boggling wealth accrued by high-profile drug lords like El Chapo Guzmán, give testament to the inescapable fact that there is a never-ending demand in the western world for marijuana, cocaine, heroin, ecstasy and other classified substances. While marijuana is increasingly tolerated, even in countries and states where it remains technically illegal, there are usually legal ramifications for those caught using or dealing 'Class A' drugs such as cocaine, heroin, LSD and ecstacy. Yet before the start of the 1960s, recreational drug use was barely a part of public consciousness outside the rarefied worlds of jazz musicians and Hollywood actors. And yet the story of our species' relationship with narcotics can be traced back to the earliest days man walked the earth.

Archaeological records tell us that psychotropic substances have always played a role in human life: they were used by healers for medicinal purposes, priests in religious ceremonies and by the civilian population in ways deemed 'acceptable' within those societies. This in itself raises the difficult question that lies at the heart of every drugs debate: which substances should be allowed and for what reasons? In the modern world, recreational drugs such as alcohol, caffeine and nicotine are largely permitted by law; cannabis is legal in some places;

opium is used in the production of critically important painkillers, but as recreational heroin it is universally outlawed; similarly, cocaine has recognized medical uses but is otherwise banned. Changes in usage and acceptability within any society do, however, take place over time: barely a century ago, young mothers were being encouraged to give heroin-laced syrup to their babies to help them sleep at night; and recent evidence would suggest that among many of the 'millennial' generation in America and western Europe smoking tobacco is increasingly taboo.

Although the second half of the 20th century saw the emergence of synthetic narcotics – those created using man-made chemicals – the three most widely used illegal drug families derive from nature itself: cocaine from the leaf of the coca plant; heroin and opium from the resin of the poppy plant; and marijuana from the leaves of the cannabis plant. Each one has its own long and fascinating history.

COCAINE

Most of the world's cocaine production takes place in South America, principally Colombia, Peru and Bolivia. And almost all of it is distributed to the United States – and to much of the rest of the world – through the trafficking routes created and run by the Mexican drug cartels.

Cocaine is derived from the leaves of the coca plant native to the Andean countries in the west of the continent. For thousands of years, indigenous South American peoples chewed the leaves of the plant, which is one of nature's oldest and most potent stimulants. This resulted in an increased heart rate, which created an energy boost that also made it easier to breathe in the high altitudes of the Andes mountains. Ancient Peruvian mummies dating back more than a thousand years have been discovered buried with the remains of coca leaves. Images found on artefacts of the period show the faces of adults with bulging cheeks as they chewed; from this we can ascertain that it was a widespread practice, especially in religious ceremonies.

Europeans first came across the plant when Spanish Conquistadores led by Francisco Pizzaro arrived in Peru in 1526. Discovering rich new channels of natural resources to exploit, the Spanish began digging silver mines and quickly discovered that when supplied with coca leaves, the indigenous Inca forced labourers were happier, worked harder and were more compliant. In 1569, Spanish botanist Nicolás Monardes noted the effect: 'When they wished to make themselves drunk and out of judgment they chewed a mixture of tobacco and coca leaves which make them go as they were out of their wittes.'

The first attempts to control the use of the coca leaf were made during the same period, as Catholic bishops in Spain's new South American colonies believed it would undermine the spread of Christianity; although it was not banned outright, restrictions were placed on the amount of land that could be used in its cultivation.

Exported to Europe, coca leaves soon found medicinal uses. Padre Blas Valera wrote in 1609: 'Coca protects the body from many ailments, and our doctors use it in powdered form to reduce the swelling of wounds, to strengthen broken bones, to expel cold from the body or prevent it from entering, and to cure rotten wounds or sores that are full of maggots. And if it does so much for outward ailments, will not its singular virtue have even greater effect in the entrails of those who eat it?'

A number of early chemists attempted to isolate the cocaine alkaloid from the coca leaf, but this was not successfully achieved until 1855 by Friedrich Gaedcke. The process was refined five years later by PhD student Albert Niemann, who wrote in his thesis: 'Its solutions have an alkaline reaction, a bitter taste, promote the flow of saliva and leave a peculiar numbness, followed by a sense of cold when applied to the tongue.' It was Niemann who named this alkaloid 'cocaine'.

Cocaine acts as a local anaesthetic, blocking sodium channels on the surface of nerve cells, so that when applied to a specific area of the body, the nearby pain-sensing nerves are temporarily prevented from transmitting pain signals to the brain. This 'numbing' effect made it exceptionally useful in surgical applications. Austrian ophthalmologist Carl Koller began to use cocaine on his patients when performing delicate surgery: after soaking the area in a cocaine solution, Koller found that they no longer flinched when the scalpel touched the eye. It was quickly adapted for use in other types of surgery. In 1884, Koller's friend Sigmund Freud, one of the celebrated early adopters of cocaine as a recreational substance, wrote *Uber Coca*, a paper he described himself as a 'song of praise to this magical substance'.

When snorted as a powder, injected as a solution or smoked, the drug raises the level of the neurotransmitter dopamine in the brain, creating a sense of euphoria, increased energy and frequently a heightened sense of self-confidence. Freud's self-experimentation was even sponsored by Parke-Davis, once America's largest drug manufacturer and now a subsidiary of pharmaceutical giant Pfizer. Freud described 'the most gorgeous excitement' and 'exhilaration and lasting euphoria' when he first ingested cocaine. Some believe cocaine might have had a significant impact on Freud's pioneering work in psychoanalysis during the same period.

Yet Freud had not bargained for one aspect of regular cocaine use. The addictive nature of the drug was already beginning to manifest itself in America, where it was being used as a treatment for opium addicts – often replacing one addiction with another. Freud, himself, would struggle for 12 years to free himself from his cocaine compulsion.

Towards the end of the century, cocaine became widely used in over-the-counter medicinal tonics. One of the most famous was inspired by a popular French mixture called Vin Mariani, a concoction of red wine and coca leaves. In 1886, John Pemberton, a former colonel in the Confederate army who was wounded and became addicted to morphine during the American Civil War, launched his own cocaine syrup tonic. He marketed the drink as a cure for indigestion, headaches, nervous disorders, impotence… and morphine addiction. At first sold only in Atlanta, a state that had recently passed alcohol prohibition legislation, it was advertised as: 'Coca-Cola: The Temperance Drink'. The recipe for

Coke has always been a closely guarded secret, but when concerns about the safety of cocaine began to emerge, the levels of coca used in the drink were reduced to 'a trace' by 1902 and removed altogether in 1929.

Cocaine use was now widespread, not only in tonic form but for injection into the bloodstream. It seems scarcely believable that in the 1890s, the famous Sears & Roebuck family shopping catalogue even offered a syringe and a tiny bottle of cocaine for $1.50. The drug also began to appear as a vice in late-Victorian fiction, most famously in Arthur Conan Doyle's Sherlock Holmes tales, where – much to the disapproval of his friend and colleague Dr Watson – the great sleuth would alleviate boredom between cases by injecting a seven-per cent solution of cocaine. Even though the drug was legal at that time, Conan Doyle – himself a physician – presented Holmes' addiction as an unequivocal weakness in what was otherwise a brilliant career.

Cocaine-based tonics were equally popular in Europe. One particular concoction – a strong mix of cocaine and caffeine – was bottled and sold as 'Forced March', promising users prolonged powers of endurance 'when undergoing continued mental strain or physical exertion'. It was used by both Ernest Shackleton and Robert Scott during their daring (and doomed) expeditions to the South Pole. Similar combinations were used in pill form by troops fighting on the Western Front during World War I. Approved by the military commanders who thought they kept troops alert as they endured the rigours of trench warfare, they became a subject of concern to the British government when their use continued after troops had returned home from duty. Cocaine would be one of the substances regulated by the British government in the 1920 Dangerous Drugs Act.

It was around this time that cocaine addiction first began to be linked with crime. Early reports in the United States were heavily racial in tone. In 1900, the *Journal of the American Medical Association* noted that 'Negroes in the South are reported as being addicted to a new form of vice – that of "cocaine sniffing" or the "coke habit".' Newspapers spread sensational stories of an epidemic of black cocaine addicts raping white women: a *New York Times* headline read: 'Negro Cocaine "Fiends" Are New Southern Menace: Murder and Insanity Increasing Among Lower-Class Blacks'. It reported that '... sexual desires are increased and perverted... peaceful negroes become quarrelsome, and timid negroes develop a degree of "Dutch courage" that is sometimes almost incredible'. Later research would reveal that black Americans had been using cocaine and opium at a significantly lower rate than their white counterparts. Nevertheless, the growing controversy led to the creation of America's first major piece of national drug legislation when the Harrison Narcotics Tax Act was passed in 1914, outlawing the sale and use of both coca and opium products unless prescribed by a doctor. The later Jones-Miller Act of 1922 placed heavy restrictions on cocaine manufacturers and, unlike heroin, for which a burgeoning black market would open, cocaine use largely disappeared.

Demand for illegal cocaine was minimal in the decades that immediately followed World War II. Until the 1970s, it generally entered the United States smuggled in the linings of suitcases by 'mules' on commercial flights or was brought into the country in small shipments on fishing trawlers from Argentina, Brazil and Chile. But as the drug became increasingly fashionable in New York and Los Angeles, Colombian traffickers, most notably the Medellín syndicate – an organization run by a former car thief and kidnapper named Pablo Escobar – gradually seized control of the supply routes.

At first Escobar sent his contraband through the Caribbean, making large shipments to the Bahamian island of Norman's Cay, where it would be transferred to small planes that could fly below US radar into Florida's Everglades. When the United States Drug Enforcement Agency closed down this route in 1982, the Medellín supply chain simply moved elsewhere. At its peak towards the end of the 1980s, Escobar was controlling up to seven flights a day into the USA or Mexico, each one carrying 500 kilos (1,100 lbs) of cocaine. The economics were startling:

a kilo would cost around $1,000 (£800) to refine and $4,000 (£3,200) to smuggle into the United States, where it could then be sold for up to $70,000 (£56,000). Little wonder that Escobar would ultimately be regarded as the wealthiest criminal in history, massively out-earning Prohibition-era mobsters like Al Capone.

As increasing amounts of Medellín cocaine passed through Mexico's drug routes, the local trafficking cartels began to assume increasing influence. In 1991, a new Colombian government came to power and, aided by the United States, moved against the Medellín cartel. Escobar died in a police shootout on 2 December 1993 and the syndicate fragmented. His rivals from the Cali cartel were also wiped out – killed or arrested – by government forces. At that point, the Mexican cartels took more or less complete control of the cocaine trade, with the Sinaloa cartel the most influential. On 23 June 1995, the Mexican army arrested Héctor Luis Palma Salazar, the senior figure within the Sinaloa, and leadership was assumed by Joaquín 'El Chapo' Guzmán Loera, who until his capture and incarceration was the single most significant figure in not only the cocaine trade but the whole, vast world of global drug trafficking.

During the 1980s, cocaine took on new form in the shape of crack cocaine. A hard, mineral-like substance, crack is created by mixing baking soda or ammonia with powdered cocaine and then applying heat to create a 'rock'. Later when reheated, the vapour is inhaled, and so reaches the brain more quickly, producing a brief but extremely intense high. Crack is far more potent and addictive than regular cocaine and has been widely associated with increased urban crime rates in the United States.

Recent evidence suggests that the Mexican cartels have strengthened their control over the cocaine business. In 2019, General Luis Ramírez, chief of Colombia's anti-drug police force, reported that instead of buying pure cocaine from producers in Columbia they were smuggling the unrefined coca paste into Mexico and refining it themselves in their own laboratories. This also makes the production of crack cocaine far more economical.

In spite of – or some might even argue aided by – the efforts of the authorities, the Mexican cartels retain an absolute grip over the global cocaine trade.

OPIATES

Both morphine and heroin are derived from the opium poppy (*Papaver somniferum*). Unripened seed pods give off a rubbery residue, which is scraped off, collected and dried. According to Buddhist folklore, the 5th-century monk Bodhidharma, after repeatedly falling asleep while attempting to meditate, tore off his eyelids in anger; where they fell to the ground, a plant sprang up that when consumed would create a sense of well-being or sleep – it was the first opium poppy. (Other versions of the myth also claim to show the origins of the tea plant.) In fact, there is plenty of evidence to suggest that opium's psychoactive properties were well known several thousand years earlier. Sumerian and Babylonian writings from 3500 BC refer to its preparation for the relief of pain or even, when combined with hemlock, to provide a quick and painless method of death. In ancient Egypt, it was used in rituals by priests and magicians; its invention was credited to the god Thoth and it was said that Isis had administered the drug to Ra to cure a severe head pain.

Opium found its way into Europe some time around the 11th century with soldiers returning from The Crusades in the Holy Land, and it would later become a popular cure-all in the early days of western medicine. Seventeenth-century pioneer Thomas Sydenham, the 'English Hippocrates', used it to treat pain, sleeplessness and diarrhoea. Such was his enthusiasm that he noted: 'Among the remedies which it has pleased Almighty God to give to man to relieve his sufferings, none is so universal and so efficacious as opium.'

In the 1660s, Sydenham also compounded an opium tincture that he named laudanum, a liquid containing small amounts of opium mixed with sherry wine, cinnamon and saffron. Thereafter, physicians and quacks alike experimented with numerous opium concoctions, mixing it with, among other substances, mercury, hashish, ether chloroform, cayenne pepper, belladonna, wine and alcohol.

Opium's most notorious side-effect, however, became all too well known in the 19th century, when a large number of those receiving treatment became addicted. In the United States, laudanum was often prescribed to women to relieve menstrual pain, and by the 1880s there were thought to be up to 200,000 addicts in America; three-quarters of those were women. Among their number was Mary Todd Lincoln, the wife of President Abraham Lincoln.

It's clear that recreational use of opium also has a lengthy lineage. One of the earliest accounts we have is in the writings of Xu Boling in 15th-century China, who noted that in addition to its medicinal properties smoking opium also 'enhances the art of alchemists, sex and court ladies'; it could also be used 'to aid masculinity, strengthen sperm and regain vigour'. For the Chinese, the strong association between opium and sex prevailed into the 20th century.

In 1573, Venetian nobleman Constantino Garzoni noted during his visit to the city of Constantinople (now Istanbul) in the Ottoman Empire that he encountered a 'black water made with opium' which intoxicated many of the natives, but to which they were so addicted that 'to go without it they will quickly die'.

In China, recreational opium use began as the preserve of the wealthy but soon became widespread. In the 18th century, opium addiction became such a problem that the emperor passed a number of decrees making the opium trade illegal. The British East India Company – effectively a private arm of the British government – began smuggling opium into China from India. Requests to stop the illegal trade were ignored. 'Opium has a harm. Opium is a poison, undermining our good customs and morality. Its use is prohibited by law,' the emperor decreed. 'Deceitful merchants buy and sell it to gain profit... If we capture violators, they should immediately be punished and the opium destroyed at once.'

The seizing of smuggled opium by the Chinese authorities sparked two Opium Wars between China and Britain during the mid-19th century, which ended with the trading of opium being legitimized. British Prime Minister William Gladstone would later describe it as 'a war more unjust in its origin, a war more calculated in its progress to cover this country with permanent disgrace'.

It was not until the communist uprising under Mao Zedong in 1949 that the production and consumption of opium in China was largely wiped out.

Laudanum addiction became a well-publicized issue in Victorian Britain. Since it was treated as a medication, it was not taxed in the same way as alcohol; this made it cheaper than gin or wine and thus it appealed to the poor. It was also famously used by a number of British literary figures. In 1797, Samuel Taylor Coleridge wrote the poem *Kubla Khan* after waking up from a dream while under the influence of opium. Coleridge had been treated with laudanum for jaundice but quickly became addicted, requiring up to 100 drops per day. Thomas De Quincey's *Confessions of an English Opium-Eater* in 1822 was the first notable published account of both the pleasures and perils of the drug. 'Oh! Heavens!' he wrote of his first experience, 'What an upheaving, from its lowest depths, of the inner spirit! What an apocalypse of the world within me!'

In its raw form, opium contains a large number of alkaloids, one of which was isolated in 1804 by German chemist Friedrich Sertürner. He named the substance *morphium* after Morpheus, the Greek god of dreams – it would later become known as morphine. Sertürner's medication was six times stronger than opium and, so he originally believed, far less addictive. Indeed, Sertürner came close to death when he first administered it to himself. He would later note: 'I consider it my duty to attract attention to the terrible effects of this new substance I called morphium in order that calamity may be averted.'

Morphine was quickly recognized as a powerful painkiller and was used extensively to treat the wounded during the American Civil War.

It was soon apparent, however, that morphine was even more addictive than opium, and it was said that during the conflict over 400,000 fell foul of what became known as 'soldier's disease' – morphine addiction.

Morphine continues to be the most powerful treatment for severe pain, such as serious injury, surgery or late-stage cancer.

Diacetylmorphine (diamorphine) was first synthesized in 1874 by British chemist C. R. Alder Wright, who combined morphine with acetic anhydride. It was found to be several times more potent and less addictive than morphine itself. German chemist Felix Hoffman repeated this experiment 23 years later while working for the Bayer pharmaceutical company in Germany, which marketed the drug as an over-the-counter alternative to morphine or codeine. The name heroin was coined based on the German word *heroisch*, meaning 'heroic' or 'strong'.

Heroin was initially considered something of a wonder drug, especially when treating respiratory diseases, but it was not long before some doctors began noticing addictive side-effects. In particular, Dr Berthold Turnauer noted how some of his patients had quickly built up a tolerance to the drug, making increasingly higher dosages necessary for continued effectiveness. As heroin-related admissions to hospital began to rise, Bayer ended production in 1913, although by this time other companies had begun manufacturing the drug. Seven years later, the House of Delegates of the American Medical Association passed a resolution banning its use altogether. In the UK, the negative effect of heroin gels used by troops in the trenches during World War I had already been noted, and in 1920 the Dangerous Drugs Act banned the over-the-counter sale of heroin – although unlike the US, the UK still made allowance for prescribed medical uses.

The recreational use of heroin emerged in the early 1910s after morphine and laudanum addicts discovered its intoxicating effects, which could be enhanced by administering it intravenously – injected into a vein. Its abuse spread quickly and by the time heroin was made illegal it had already become a major crime stimulus in many American cities as addicts stole to bankroll their habits. In 1924, almost all criminal drug-users arrested in New York City were heroin addicts.

Changes in the law and international treaties were effective in restricting the use of heroin, which had decreased dramatically by the beginning of the 1930s. But as with the Prohibition years in America, the criminal underworld stepped in, producing and trafficking heroin to meet a continuing demand. Most of the original heroin labs were based around Shanghai and Tianjin in China and run by Chinese triad gangs, which controlled its export west into Turkey. The so-called French Connection, headed by Paul Carbone and the Corsican mafia, smuggled the heroin further west through Europe to the French port of Marseilles and then on to New York City. Meanwhile, the Mafia had begun to take advantage of the chaos in post-war Italy to set up their own production facilities, using much the same routes to reach the United States.

The large-scale production of heroin in China ended with the victory of the Communists in the civil war in 1949. Producers and dealers were executed, opium-producing regions were planted with new crops and 10 million addicts were ordered into compulsory treatment. This massive new gap in the market was quickly filled as production shifted south to the 'Golden Triangle' of Myanmar, Thailand and Laos, which produced most of the world's heroin for the next four decades.

Since the 1980s, the majority of the world's heroin has been produced within the 'Golden Crescent', covering Afghanistan, Iran and Pakistan. Between 2001 and 2007, opium production in Afghanistan alone accelerated from 180 tons to more than 8,000 tons. Heroin leaves the region through Turkey on the 'Balkan route' or departs Northern Afghanistan for Central Asia on its way to Russia – what is often called the 'smack track'.

As far as the United States is concerned, the Mexican drug cartels have almost total control over the heroin that enters the country. Although poppy cultivation is now illegal in both Mexico and Colombia, it has a long tradition among some of the poorest rural districts, including

El Chapo Guzmán's home territory of Sinaloa. Indeed, his father, Emilio Guzmán Bustillos, although officially a cattle rancher, was thought to have been a *gomero* – an opium poppy farmer. With limited opportunities to make a legitimate living, his sons naturally followed suit.

By 2019, according to the US Drug Enforcement Agency, 91 per cent of heroin seized had entered the country from Mexico, primarily cultivated in the hills of Guerrero state, some 800 miles (1,290 km) south of the United States-Mexican border. After decades of covert involvement in the drugs trade, the Mexican government took an aggressive military stance on the heroin market in the 21st century, launching destructive raids on areas in which the opium poppy was grown. In spite of efforts to convince rural farmers to switch to producing corn and other legal crops, the demand for heroin in the United States ensured that opium cultivation – in spite of its attendant risks – remained vastly more profitable. Rural poverty remains such that many farmers could see only two alternatives: grow poppies or illegally cross the US border to find employment.

In recent times, use of opioids like heroin in the United States has soared, mainly in the form of powerful legally prescribed pain relief medication such as fentanyl, oxycodone, hydrocodone and tramadol. These drugs are widely regarded as having been over-prescribed by medical professionals during the 1990s, leaving many who were given the drugs in good faith with severe addiction problems, and fuelling a black market among users whose legal prescriptions had been stopped. In some cases, where supply no longer existed, users turned to the heroin market. Between 2010 and 2013, deaths from heroin overdoses tripled in the USA; this significant jump included many who had 'crossed over' from prescription painkillers.

CANNABIS

Like the coca leaf and the opium poppy, the cannabis plant has also been ingested by humans for many thousands of years. Indigenous to

Central Asia and the Indian subcontinent since Neolithic times, cannabis was used in the production of rope in China and Japan. Its psychoactive use, achieved by inhaling the smoke of its burning leaves, is believed to have been part of ritual ceremonies among Indo-European tribes dating back to 3500 BC. The ancient Assyrians referred to this as *qunubu*, which literally means 'way to produce smoke' and is most likely to have been origin of the word 'cannabis'. Shamans in Thrace used it to induce trance-like states among their followers who were even known as *kabnobatai* ('those who walk on smoke').

The use of hashish – cannabis resin – spread to the Arab world during the 13th century, primarily into Egypt, from where it spread to Africa and India. During this time, and until the 1500s, cannabis was mainly consumed as an edible; it was not until the introduction of tobacco from the New World that smoking the cannabis leaves became more common.

One early western account of cannabis use came from British merchant sailor Thomas Bowery in 1673. Visiting Machilitipatnam on India's Coromandel Coast, he noted that while the Muslim merchant community did not partake 'in any Stronge drinke... they find means to besot themselves Enough with *Bangha*... not one of them faith to intoxicate them in admiration'. Bhang has been used in the Indian subcontinent since 1000 BC and is prepared by crushing the leaves and buds of the cannabis plant and mixing them with food or drink. Reporting the experiences of his crew, Bowery wrote that those that drank the concoction became 'merry at that instant...' and would 'Continue She with Exceedinge great laughter... laughinge heartily at Every thinge they discerne'.

[AUTHOR NOTE: The spellings and seemingly random capitalizations are from the original 17th-century text.]

By the 19th century, recreational use of cannabis throughout the world was relatively common, much of its spread attributable to the major European colonial powers. In 1798, during Napoleon's invasion of Egypt, an Islamic country where alcohol was not available or permitted, French troops began a widespread use of hashish; it became so problematic that Napoleon banned its use from his armies shortly after the end of the campaign. Although this was not the first attempt to control its use – the Arabian Emir Soudon Sheikouni had outlawed cannabis and ordered the destruction of crops as early as 1300 – governments began to assess its impact. The British Indian government was the first to carry out a detailed study of cannabis before concluding in 1894 that 'its effect on society is rarely appreciable', and that 'moderate use practically produces no ill effects'. By the end of the century, however, cannabis had been outlawed in much of the Islamic world.

In the mid-19th century, the Western medical world began to investigate other potential uses for cannabis. It was an Irish physician, William Brooke O'Shaughnessy, working for the East India Company, who first undertook extensive research into the medicinal properties of cannabis. His findings led him to believe that, among other benefits, it could be used for effective pain relief, migraines and to stop convulsions in infants. (Its uses in conditions such as epilepsy are now widely accepted.) During the same period, French psychiatrist Jacques-Joseph Moreau (widely known as 'Moreau de Tours') studied the effects of cannabis on melancholia, leading to the publication of his pioneering work *Du Hachisch et de l'aliénation mentale (Hashish and Mental Illness)*.

As was the case with cocaine and opium, cannabis was used during the second half of the 19th century in an assortment of widely available patent medicines, over 2,000 varieties being produced by 280 manufacturers. And their target markets were also sometimes surprising: a Scandinavian cannabis-malt concoction was promoted as 'an excellent lunch drink, especially for children and young people'.

In one of the first examples of hard-hitting investigative journalism, many of these medicines were shown to be 'snake oil' remedies sold by quacks. Samuel Hopkins Adams' 1905 exposé, *The Great American Fraud*, sold more than a half a million copies. Along with the growing recognition of the harmful addictive nature of opium and cocaine remedies, its influence led directly to the US government passing the 1906 Pure Food and Drug Act, which placed restrictions on the use of narcotics. In Britain, cannabis was added to the Dangerous Drugs Act in 1928, effectively outlawing its use.

By the 1920s, cannabis had become more widely known in America by its Spanish name, marijuana. Its popularity during and beyond the Prohibition era can be charted by the mainstream popularity of 'reefer songs' such as Benny Goodman's 'Texas Tea Party' and Cab Calloway's 'Reefer Man'. At the same time, sensationalist newspaper headlines detailing drug busts in Hollywood and the music business fuelled growing concerns about the impact of marijuana on America's youth. Morality films of the 1930s, such as *Assassin of Youth* and *Reefer Madness* – both now viewed as unintentionally hilarious cult period pieces – added to pressure from religious groups for firm nationwide action to be taken. The Federal Bureau of Narcotics was set up by the US government in 1930 as part of its official policy to outlaw all recreational drugs; their work led to the Marihuana Tax Act of 1937, which effectively made possession and trade in the drug illegal outside legitimate medical uses.

A lucrative black market quickly emerged for the drug in the United States – largely controlled by the Mafia and later the Mexican cartels – and its recreational use grew to a point where, by the 1960s, it was a commonplace part of America's counterculture. Concerns grew as it became broadly socially acceptable. In 1971 President Nixon privately acknowledged that he knew 'the arguments that it was no worse than whiskey... as far as legalizing [marijuana] is concerned I think we've got to take a strong stand.' He, and many like him, saw it as a moral issue. 'Do you think the Russians allow dope? Hell no... you see, homosexuality, dope, immorality in general: these are the enemies of strong societies.' And thus began America's War on Drugs.

By the end of the 20th century, marijuana had become almost mainstream. Although at this time recreational use was still technically illegal, laws in many countries were either relaxed or not enforced. In the Netherlands, the sale of cannabis in cafés has been tolerated since the 1970s, and although listed in the UK as a Class B drug, personal possession is only likely to result in prosecution if the user is smoking openly in public. In 2013, in an attempt to cut crime, Uruguay became the first country to fully legalize the recreational use of cannabis. Canada followed suit in 2018. Spain, Portugal, Switzerland and South Africa also make legal allowances for personal use. The situation in America varies from state to state: in Alaska, California, Colorado, Illinois, Maine, Massachusetts, Michigan, Nevada, Oregon, Vermont and Washington, recreational use of marijuana is legally allowed; only in Idaho, South Dakota and Nebraska is it outlawed; in the remaining states it is legal for medical uses or else it is decriminalized.

It seems highly likely that laws relating to cannabis will continue to become increasingly lenient throughout the world.

METHAMPHETAMINE

Known as 'meth', 'crystal meth' or 'ice', methamphetamine comes in crystal chunks or shiny blue-white rocks and is usually smoked using a small glass pipe; it can also be swallowed, snorted or injected into the vein. The drug stimulates the central nervous system, with a rush of euphoria shortly after it's been administered. Dopamine floods the parts of the brain that regulate feelings of pleasure. Users may also feel confident and energetic. The 'rush' is an extremely powerful sensation, which is why it can easily become such an addictive substance. As with other drugs, tolerance builds up with continued usage, so users will require higher doses to achieve the same effects. It is a popular party drug because it has been reported as increasing sexual desire and prolonging sexual activity.

Although the recreational use of methamphetimine before the 1970s was relatively rare, its history dates back to the end of the 19th century when amphetamine was synthesized. In 1919, Japanese pharmacologist

Akira Ogata first synthesized methamphetamine hydrochloride from a reduction of ephedrine, red phosphorus and iodine. During World War II, methamphetamine was produced in tablet form in Germany under the name Pervitin and was widely used by the military as a stimulant to keep soldiers and pilots alert and awake. Use was so common that pills were known colloquially as *Stuka-Tabletten* (after the Luftwaffe dive bomber aircraft) or *Hermann-Göring Pills* (after the commander-in-chief of the Luftwaffe). In the 1960s, it was used legally as a weight-loss treatment. Under the brand name Obitrol, it became a popular diet pill in the United States; it was withdrawn in 1973 after the addictive nature of methamphetamine became known. There are few legitimate medical uses for which methamphetamine can be prescribed – in some cases, it may be used to treat obesity and attention deficit hyperactivity disorder (ADHD). In its modern recreational form, methamphetamine is considerably more potent.

The appeal of meth to criminal groups is that it is easy to produce and the profit margins are enormous. In the 1970s, it was largely distributed by biker gangs, but by the end of the 1980s production and trafficking were largely controlled by the Mexican cartels, in particular El Chapo Guzmán's Sinaloa organization. Most commercial methamphetamine is produced in enormous 'superlab' complexes, but with skill and the right equipment it can also created in a normal household kitchen. The precursor chemical used in meth is ephedrine or pseudoephedrine, which is also found in some cold medicines, and is used by 'home cooks'.

Methamphetamine was generally regarded as an underground drug, relatively unknown to the general public. Mainstream awareness came in 2008 with the TV series *Breaking Bad*, about a high school teacher diagnosed with terminal cancer who uses his expertise in chemistry to build a 'meth kitchen' to provide for his family after his death.

APPENDIX D:

STREET SLANG

Since the time that certain narcotics were first outlawed during the 1920s, specific drugs have been known under a variety of slang street names. These were sometimes used as a way of being able to buy or sell illegal narcotics without risking being overheard using their real names. When *Time* magazine first published an article on marijuana in 1943, the alternative terminologies were already well developed: 'To its users, the drug has many names… marijuana may be called muggles, mooter, Mary Warner, Mary Jane, Indian hay, loco weed, love weed, bambalacha, mohasky, mu, moocah, grass, tea or blue sage. Cigarettes made from it are killers, goof-butts, joy-smokes, giggle-smokes or reefers.' A few of these have made it through to the present day, but numerous others have been added along the way. Britain's police forces have been issued with a list of more than 3,000 street names for illegally traded narcotics; in 2018, the United States Drug Enforcement Agency issued its own exhaustive 125-page document, with well over 500 known names for cocaine alone.

COCAINE

7; 62; 77; 777; 921; A-1; Adidas; All-American Drug; Ancla; Angel Powder; Angie; Animals; Apache; Apodo; Arriba; Audi; Aunt Nora; Azucar; Baby Powder; Barrato; Basuco; Bazooka (cocaine paste mixed with marijuana);

Beach; Belushi (cocaine mixed with heroin); Bernice; Bernie's Flakes; Bernie's Gold Dust; Big Bird; Big Bloke; Big C; Big Flake; Big Rush; Billie Hoke; Bird; Birdie Powder; Blanca Nieves; Blanco; Blast; Blizzard; Blonde; Blocks; Blow; BMW; Board; Bobo; Bolitas; Bolivian Marching Powder; Bombita (cocaine mixed with heroin); Booger Sugar; Bose; Bouncing Powder; Brisa; Bump; C-Dust; Caballo; Caca; Cadillac; California Pancakes; Calves; Canelon; Candy; Carney; Carrie Nation; Cars; Case; Cebolla; Cecil; Cement; Charlie; Chevy; Cheyenne; Chica; Chicanitas; Chinos; Chiva; Cielo; Clear Kind; Clear Tires; Coca; Coca-Cola; Cocazo; Coconut; Coke; Cola; Colorado; Comida; Comida Dulce; Connie; Cookie; Cosa; Coso; Cosos; Crow; Crusty Treats; Cuadro; Death Valley; Designer Jeans; Devil's Dandruff; Diamonds; Diente; Dienton; Diesel; Diosa Blanca; Dona Blanca; Double Bubble; Double Letters; Dove; Dream; Dulces; Duracell; Durazno; Duro; Dust; Escama; Escorpino; Falopa; Fef1; Fichas; Fiesta; Fire (cocaine base); Fish (liquid cocaine); Fish Scale; Flake; Flea Market Jeans; Florida Snow; Flour; Food; Foolish Powder; Fox; Freeze; Friskie Powder; Frula; Funtime; Gabacho; Galaxy; Gallos; Gato; Gift of the Sun; Gin; Girl; Girlfriend; Glad Stuff; Gold Dust; Green Gold; Gringa; Gringito; Grout; Guerillo; Gueros; Guitar; H1; Hai Hit; Hamburger; Happy Dust; Happy Powder; Happy Trails; Heaven; Heaven Dust; Heavy One; Hen; Henry VIII; HH; HHJ; High Heat; HMH; Hooter; Hundai; Hunter; Ice Cream; Icing; Inca Message; Izzy; Jam; Jaime Blanco; Jaula; Jeep; Jelly; John Deere; Joy Flakes; Joy Powder; Juguetes; Jump Rope; Junk; K13; King's Habit; Kordell; La Familia; Lady; Lady Snow; Late Night; Lavada; Leaf; Libreta; Line; Loaf; Love Affair; LV; Maca Flour; Madera; Mama Coca; Mandango; Manita; Maradona; Marbol; Material; Mayback (62 grams); Mayo; Melcocha; Media Lata; Mercedes; Milk; Milonga; Mojo; Mona Lisa; Monte; Morro; Mosquitos; Movie Star Drug; Muchacha; Muebles; Mujer; Napkin; Nieve; Niña; Normal; Nose Candy; Nose Powder; Old Lady; Oyster Stew; Paint; Paloma; Paleta; Palomos; Pantalones; Papas; Paradise; Paradise White; Parrot; Pearl; Pedrito; Perico; Personal; Peruvian; Peruvian Flake; Peruvian Lady; Pescado; Peta; Pez; Pichicata; Pillow;

Pimp; Pingas; Pingos; Pintura Blanca; Poli; Pollo; Polvo; Powder; Powder Diamonds; Puma; Puritain; Quadros; Queso Blanco; Racehorse Charlie; Rambo; Refresco; Refrescas; Regular Kind; Regular Work; Reindeer Dust; Richie; Rims; Rocky Mountain; Rolex; Rolex HH; Rooster; Scale; Schmeck; Schoolboy; Scorpion; Scottie; Seed; Serpico; Sierra; Shirt; Ski Equipment; Sleigh Ride; Sneeze; Sniff; Snow; Snow Bird; Snow Cone; Snow White; Snowball; Snowflake; Society High; Soda; Soditas; Soft; Space (cocaine mixed with PCP); Special; Speedball (cocaine mixed with heroin); Stardust; Star Spangled Powder; Studio Fuel; Suave; Sugar; Superman; Sweet Stuff; Tabique; Tablas; Talco; Talquito; Tamales; Taxi; Tecate; Teenager; Teeth; Tequila; Thunder; Tire; Tonto; Toot; Tortes; Tortuga; Toyota; T-Shirts; Tubo; Tucibi (pink variety); Turkey; Tutti-Frutti; Vaquita; Wash; Wet; Whack (cocaine mixed with PCP); White; White Bitch; White Cross; White Dove; White Girl; White Goat; White Horse; White Lady; White Mercedes Benz; White Mosquito; White Paint; White Powder; White Rock; White Root; White Shirt; White T; White Wall Tires; Whitey; Whiz Bang; Wings; Wooly; Work; Yayo; Yeyo; Yoda; Zapato; Zip.

CRACK COCAINE

51s; 151s; 501s; Apple Jack; Baby T; Base; Baseball; Bazooka; Beam Me Up; Beautiful Boulders; Beemer; Bill Blass; Bings; BJ; Black Rock; Blowcaine; Blowout; Blue; Bobo; Bolo; Bomb; Bone Crusher; Bone; Boo-Boo; Boulder; Boy; Breakfast of Champions; Bubble Gum; Bullion; Bump; Candy; Caps; Casper the Ghost; Caviar; CD; Cheap Basing; Chewies; Chingy; Clicker; Climax; Cloud; Cloud Nine; Cookies; CRC; Crib; Crunch and Munch; Devil; Devil Smoke; Dice; Dime Special; Dirty Basing; Dirty Fentanyl (crack cocaine mixed with fentanyl); Double Yoke; Durin; Eastside Player; Egg; Eye Opener; Famous Dimes; Fat Bags; Fifty-One; Fish Scales; Freebase; French Fries; Garbage Rock; Geek; Glo; Gold; Golf Ball; Gravel; Great White Hope; Grit; Groceries; Hail; Hamburger Helper; Hard; Hotcakes; Hubba; Ice; Ice Cubes; Issues; Jelly Beans; Johnson; Kangaroo; Kokoma; Kryptonite; Love; Mixed Jive; Moon Rock; Nickle; Nuggets; One-Fifty-One;

Paste; Pebbles; Pee Wee; Piedras; Pile; Pony; Primo; Quarters; Raw; Ready Rock; Red Caps; RIP (Rest in Peace); Roca; Rock; Rock Attack; Rocks of Hell; Rocky III; Rooster; Rox; Roxanne; Roz; Schoolcraft; Scotty; Scramble; Scruples; Seven-Up; Sherms; Sight Ball; Slab; Sleet; Smoke; Speed Boat; Square Time Bomb; Stone; Sugar Block; Takeover (crack cocaine mixed with fentanyl); Teeth; Tension; Tissue; Top Gun; Troop; Ultimate; Up; Uzi; Wave; White Ball; White Ghost; White Sugar; White Tornado; Wrecking Crew; Yahoo; Yale; Yimyom.

FENTANYL

Apache; Birria (fentanyl mixed with heroin); Blonde; Blue Diamond; Blue Dolphin; Blues; Butter; China Girl; China Town; China White; Chinese; Chinese Buffet; Chinese Food; Crazy; Crazy One; Dance Fever; Dragon; Dragon's Breath; F; Food; Freddy; Facebook (fentanyl mixed with heroin in pill form); Fent; Fenty; Fire; Friend; Girl; Goodfella; Great Bear; Gray Stuff; He-Man; Heineken; Huerfanito; Humid; Jackpot; King Ivory; Lollipop; Murder 8; Nal; Nil; Nyl; Opes; Pharmacy; Poison; Shoes; Snowflake; Tango and Cash; TNT; Toe Tag Dope; White Girl; White Ladies.

HEROIN

Abajo; A-Bomb (heroin mixed with marijuana); Achivia; Adormidera; Amarilla; Anestesia de Caballo (heroin mixed with the horse anesthetic xylazine); Antifreeze; Apodo; Arpon; Aunt Hazel; Avocado; Azucar; Bad Seed; Baja Corte (diluted heroin); Ballot; Basketball; Basura; Beast; Beyonce; Big Bag; Big H; Big Harry; Bird; Birdie Powder; Birria; Birria Blanca; Black; Black Bitch; Black Goat; Black Olives; Black Paint; Black Pearl; Black Sheep; Black Shirt; Black Tar; Blanco; Blue; Blow Dope; Blue Hero; Bombita (heroin mixed with cocaine); Bombs Away; Bonita; Boy; Bozo; Brea Negra; Brick Gum; Brown; Brown Crystal; Brown Rhine; Brown Sugar; Bubble Gum; Burrito; Butter; Caballo; Caballo Negro; Caca; Café; Cajeta; Capital H; Cardio (white heroin); Carga; Caro; Cement; Certificada (pure heroin); Chapopote; Charlie; Charlie Horse;

Chavo; Cheese; Chicle; Chiclosa; China; China Blanca (white heroin); China Cat; China White; Chinese Buffet (white heroin); Chinese Food; Chinese Red; Chip; Chiva; Chiva Blanca; Chiva Loca (heroin mixed with fentanyl); Chiva Negra; Chivones; Chocolate; Chocolate Balls; Chocolate Shake; Choko; Chorizo; Churro Negro; Chutazo; Coco; Coffee; Cohete; Comida; Crown Crap; Curley Hair; Dark; Dark Girl; Dark Kind; Dead on Arrival (DOA); Diesel; Dirt; Dog Food; Doggie; Doojee; Dope; Dorado; Down; Downtown; Dragon; Dreck; Dynamite; Dyno; El Diablo; Engines; Enrique Grande; Esquina; Esquinilla; Fairy Dust; Flea Powder; Food (white heroin); Foolish Powder; Galloping Horse; Gamot; Gato; George Smack; Girl; Globo (balloon of heroin); Goat; Golden Girl; Good and Plenty; Good H; Goofball (heroin mixed with methamphetamine); Goma; Gorda; Gras; Grasin; Gravy; Gum; H; H-Caps; Hairy; Hard Candy; Hard One; Harry; Hats; Hazel; Heaven Dust; Heavy; Helen; Helicopter; Hell Dust; Henry; Hercules; Hero; Him; Hombre; Horse; Hot Dope; Huera; Hummers; Jojee; Joy Flakes; Joy Powder; Junk; Kabayo; Karachi; Karate; King's Tickets; La Tierra; Lemonade; Lenta; Lifesaver; Manteca; Marias; Marrion; Mayo; Mazpan; Meal; Menthol; Mexican Brown; Mexican Food (black tar heroin); Mexican Horse; Mexican Mud; Mexican Treat; Modelo Negra; Mojo; Mole; Mongega; Morena; Morenita; Mortal Combat; Motors; Mud; Mujer; Murcielago; Muzzle; Nanoo; Negra; Negra Tomasa; Negrita; Nice and Easy; Night; Noise; Obama; Old Steve; Pants; Patty; Peg; P-Funk; Piezas; Plata; Poison; Polvo; Polvo de Alegria; Polvo de Estrellas; Polvo Feliz; Poppy; Powder; Prostituta Negra; Puppy; Pure; Rambo; Raw (uncut heroin); Red Chicken; Red Eagle; Reindeer Dust; Roofing Tar; Ruby; Sack; Salt; Sand; Scag; Scat; Schmeck; Scramble (uncut heroin); Sheep; Shirts; Shoes; Skag; Skunk; Slime; Smack; Smeck; Snickers; Soda; Speedball (heroin mixed with cocaine); Spider Blue; Sticky Kind; Stufa; Sugar; Sweet Jesus; Tan; Tar; Tecata; Thunder; Tires; Tomasa; Tootsie Roll; Tragic Magic; Trees; Turtle; Vidrio; Weights; Whiskey; White; White Boy; White Girl; White Junk; White Lady; White Nurse; White Shirt; White Stuff; Wings; Witch; Witch Hazel; Zapapote.

MARIJUANA

420; A-Bomb (marijuana mixed with heroin); Acapulco Gold; Acapulco Red; Ace; African Black; African Bush; Airplane; Alfalfa; Alfombra; Alice B Toklas; All-Star; Almohada; Angola; Animal Cookies (hydroponic); Arizona; Ashes; Aunt Mary; AZ; Baby; Bale; Bambalachacha; Barbara Jean; Bareta; Bash; Bazooka (marijuana mixed with cocaine paste); BC Budd; Bernie; Bhang; Big Pillows; Biggy; Bionic (marijuana mixed with PCP); Black Bart; Black Gold; Black Maria; Blondie; Blue Cheese; Blue Crush; Blue Dream; Blue Jeans; Blue Sage; Blueberry; Bobo Bush; Boo; Boom; Branches; Broccoli; Bud; Budda; Burritos Verdes; Bush; Cabbage; Café; Cajita; Cali; Camara; Canadian Black; Catnip; Cheeba; Chernobyl; Cheese; Chicago Black; Chicago Green; Chippie; Chistosa; Christmas Tree; Chronic; Churro; Cigars; Citrol; Cola; Colorado Cocktail; Cookie (hydroponic); Cotorritos; Crazy Weed; Creeper Bud; Crippy; Crying Weed; Culican; Dank; Devils's Lettuce; Dew; Diesel; Dimba; Dinkie Dow; Diosa Verde; Dirt Grass; Ditch Weed; Dizz; Djamba; Dody; Dojo; Domestic; Donna Juana; Doobie; Downtown Brown; Drag Weed; Dro (hydroponic); Droski (hydroponic); Dry High; Elefante Pata; Endo; Escoba; Fattie; Fine Stuff; Fire; Flower; Flower Tops; Fluffy; Fuzzy Lady; Gallina; Gallito; Garden; Garifa; Gauge; Gangster; Ganja; Gash; Gato; Ghana; Gigi (hydroponic); Giggle Smoke; Giggle Weed; Girl Scout Cookies (hydroponic); Gloria; Gold; Gold Leaf; Gold Star; Gong; Good Giggles; Gorilla; Gorilla Glue; Grand Daddy Purp; Grass; Grasshopper; Green; Green Crack; Green-Eyed Girl; Green Eyes; Green Goblin; Green Goddess; Green Mercedes Benz; Green Paint; Green Skunk; Greenhouse; Grenuda; Greta; Guardada; Gummy Bears; Gunga; Hairy Ones; Hash; Hawaiian; Hay; Hemp; Herb; Hierba; Holy Grail; Homegrown; Hooch; Hoja; Humo; Hydro; Indian Boy; Indian Hay; Jamaican Gold; Jamaican Red; Jane; Jive; Jolly Green; Jon-Jem; Joy Smoke; Juan Valdez; Juanita; Jungle Juice; Kaff; Kali; Kaya; KB; Kentucky Blue; KGB; Khalifa; Kiff; Killa; Kilter; King Louie; Kona Gold; Kumba; Kush; Laughing Grass; Laughing Weed; Leaf; Lechuga; Lemon-Lime; Leña; Liamba; Lime Pillows; Little Green Friends; Little Smoke; Llesca; Loaf; Lobo; Loco

Weed; Loud; Love Nuggets; Love Weed; Lucas; M.J.; Machinery; Macoña; Mafafa; Magic Smoke; Manhattan Silver; Manteca; Maracachafa; Maria; Marimba; Mariquita; Mary Ann; Mary Jane; Mary Jones; Mary Warner; Mary Weaver; Matchbox; Matraca; Maui Wowie; Meg; Method; Mersh; Mexican Brown; Mexicali Haze; Mexican Green; Mexican Red; MMJ; Mochie (hydroponic); Moña; Monte; Moocah; Mootie; Mora; Morisqueta; Mostaza; Mota; Mother; Mowing the Lawn; Muggie; My Brother; Narizona; Northern Lights; Nug; O-Boy; OG; O.J.; Owl; Paja; Palm; Paloma; Palomita; Panama Cut; Panama Gold; Panama Red; Pakalolo; Parsley; Pasto; Pasture; Peliroja; Pelosa; Phoenix; Pine; Pink Panther; Pintura; Plant; Platinum Cookies (hydroponic); Platinum Jack; Pocket Rocket; Popcorn; Porro; Pot; Pretendo; Prop 215; Puff; Purple Haze; Purple OG; Queen Ann's Lace; Red Hair; Ragweed; Railroad Weed; Rainy Day Woman; Rasta Weed; Red Cross; Red Dirt; Reefer; Reggie; Repollo; Righteous Bush; Root; Rope; Rosa Maria; Salt and Pepper; Santa Marta; Sasafras; Sativa; Shoes; Sinsemilla; Shmagma; Shora; Shrimp; Shwag; Skunk; Skywalker (hydroponic); Smoke; Smoochy Woochy Poochy; Smoke Canada; Sour OG; Spliff; Stems; Sticky; Stink Weed; Sugar Weed; Sweet Lucy; Tahoe (hydroponic); Tangy OG; Terp; Terpenes; Tex-Mex; Texas Tea; Tigitty; Tila; Tims; Top Shelf; Tosca; Train Wreck; Trees; Trinity OG; Tweeds; Valle; Wake and Bake; Weed; Weed Tea; Wet (marijuana dipped in PCP); Wheat; White-Haired Lady; Wooz; Yellow Submarine; Yen Pop; Yerba; Yesca; Young Girls; Zacate; Zacatecas; Zambi; Zip; Zoom (marijuana mixed with PCP).

METHAMPHETAMINE

Accordion; Amp; Aqua; Arroz; Assembled (crystal meth); Batu; Begok; Biker's Coffee; Blue; Blue Bell Ice Cream; Beers; Bottles; Bucio; Bud Light; Bump; Cajitas; Chalk; Chandelier; Chavalone; Chicken; Chicken Feed; Chicken Powder; Chris; Christine; Christy; Clear; Clothing Cleaner; Cold; Cold One; Colorado Rockies; Crank; Cream; Cri-Cri; Crink; Crisco; Crissy; Christy; Crypto; Crystal; Cuadro; Day; Diamond; Dunk; El Gata Diablo; Evil Sister; Eye Glasses; Fire; Fizz; Flowers; Foco; Food; Frio; Fruit; Gak; Garbage;

G-Funk; Gifts; Girls; Glass; Go-Fast; Go-Go; Goofball (methamphetamine mixed with heroin); Groceries; Hard Ones; Hare; Hawaiian Salt; Hielo; Hiropon; Hot Ice; Hubbers; Ice; Ice Cream; Ice Water; Icehead; Jale; Jug of Water; L.A. Glass; L.A. Ice; Lemons; Lemon Drop; Light; Light Beige; Livianas; Madera; Mamph; Meth; Methlies Quick; Mexican Crack; Mexican Crank; Miss Girl; Montura; Motor; Muchacha; Nails; One Pot; No-Doze; Paint; Pantalones; Patudas; Peanut Butter Crank; Piñata; Pointy Ones; Pollito; Popsicle; Purple; Raspado; Rims; Rocket Fuel; Salt; Shabu; Shards; Shatter; Shaved Ice; Shiny Girl; Small Girl; Soap Dope; Soft Ones; Speed; Speed Dog; Spicy Kind; Spin; Stove Top; Stuff; Super Ice; Table; Tina; Tires; Trash; Truck; Tupperware; Tweak; Unassembled (powder meth); Uppers; Ventanas; Vidrio; Walking Zombie; Water; Wazz; White; Whizz; Windows; Witches Teeth; Yaba; Yellow Barn; Yellow Cake; Yellow Kind; Zip.

INDEX